CHAPLAIN MOSES

What Chaplains Can Learn from Moses

Kenneth W. Cook

ISBN 978-1-63961-879-8 (paperback)
ISBN 978-1-63961-880-4 (digital)

Christian Faith Publishing, Inc.
832 Park Avenue
Meadville, PA 16335
www.christianfaithpublishing.com

Scripture references are from the Holy Bible, New International Version.

Some accounts of individuals have been modified to ensure the identity of the person cannot be discovered.

Printed in the United States of America

CONTENTS

ACKNOWLEDGMENTS

I want to thank the following people who have contributed their insights:

Chaplain Richard Dayringer, for believing that I could become an effective chaplain.

Chaplain (COL) Matthew McGowan, for urging me to take the long view and not resign from the Army Reserve when busily pursuing my doctorate.

Rev. Dan Scott, my pastor, for visiting me at every setting I served except one. His availability to listen to me for twenty-five years helped me find perspective. He thoroughly grasped the value of chaplain ministry.

Lynn Cook Dobbs and Julie Cook Faught, for checking grammar, spelling, punctuation, etc.

Randy Cook, for extensive suggestions regarding the transitions and flow.

Tim Cook, for the drawings of Moses' face.

Mike Dobbs, for proofreading.

Martha Cook, for deciphering my scrawl and typing numerous revisions. Most of all, I appreciate her encouragement.

INTRODUCTION

Moses, My Hero

M oses is my hero. I discovered a deep appreciation of Moses through a song I heard in the 1970s. The song called "Moses" was composed by Ken Medema and sung by him at Carson Newman College. The singing was inspiring, and the words were relevant.

The words are courtesy of Word Music Inc.[1]

Moses

Old Moses, way back there in the wilderness. Saw some smoke, came to the bush, and the bush was burning. God said, "Take off your shoes, Moses, you're on holy ground. Moses, I've chosen you to be my man. Moses, way down in Egypt's land. Moses, I've chosen you to work for me. Moses, I've chosen you to set my people free."

"Not me, Lord! Don't you know I can't talk so good? I stutter all the time. Do you know my brother, Aaron? He can sing like an angel, talk like a preacher. Not me, Lord! I can't talk so good, and another thing, how will they know that I've been here with you? How will they know what you've sent me to do?

Don't you know in Egypt they want little Moses' head? Don't you know in Egypt they want little Moses dead? Don't you know they'll never hear a single word I say? Maybe you better get your dirty work done another way. Not me, Lord!"

"What's in your hand, Moses?"

"It's just a rod."

"Throw it down, Moses."

"You mean like on the ground?"

"Yes, I said throw it down, Moses."

"Lord, don't take my rod away from me. Don't you know it's my only security? Don't you know when you live here all alone a man's gotta have something he can call his own. Not me, Lord!"

"Throw it down, Moses!"

"But, Lord, I…"

"Throw it down, Moses"

Moses threw the rod on the ground and the rod became a hissing snake.

Well Moses started running! Well maybe you'd run! Well maybe I'd run.

He was running from a hot rod. Running from a hissing snake. Running scared of what God's gonna do. Running scared he'll get ahold of you.

And the Lord said, "Stop! Pick it up by the tail."

"Lord, you have not been here very long. Lord, you've got the whole thing wrong. Don't you know that you never pick up a hissing snake by his…"

"Pick it up Moses!"

Oh, God, it's a rod again! It's a rod again!

"Do you know what it means, Moses? The rod of Moses became the rod of God. With the rod of God, strike the rock and the water will come. With the rod of God part the waters of the sea. With the rod of God you can strike old Pharaoh dead. With the rod of God you can set the people free. Do you know what I'm trying to say, Moses?"

What do you hold in your hand this day? To whom or to what are you bound? Are you willing to give it to God right now? Give it up! Let it go! Throw it down!

Medema's depiction of the burning bush event when God confronted Moses identified four critical issues. Ministers must consider these same issues when planning a career in chaplaincy. Issues from the song included surrender to God's will, God's power to make things happen in unexpected ways, the use of personal skills already present, and awareness that God will continue to guide and direct.

1. Surrendering to God was a necessary first step in the process. Surrendering usually portrays a negative, unwelcome event as when a soldier is captured. Another side of surrender can be seen. Voluntarily giving up something, even something highly valued, is a form of surrender. Moses gave up the solitary, maybe peaceful life of a shepherd. He strongly resisted this surrender but eventually relented. Doing what God wanted rather than what Moses wanted set the stage for following God's leadership. He turned his life and his work over to God. For the rest of his life, Moses strived to do what God wanted him to do. This focus became his primary motivation.

2. God demonstrated His dynamic power through a bush burned but not consumed. Moses quickly recognized that he would not have the power, skills, insights, energy, and other attributes to accomplish this mission. God's power would make the difference. Moses, having seen his rod change, gained strong confidence that God could act in unexpected ways.

3. A rod was an important possession to every man in Moses' time. Rods were the essential tool for shepherds. The shepherd's rod and staff enabled him to control, guide, and protect the sheep. A rod symbolized power and authority. Moses' rod would become instrumental in future events, such as striking a rock with the rod to get water at Mount Horeb (Exodus 17:3–6).

4. Moses witnessed the power of God and became fully convinced of God's actions. He had no idea of the numerous additional ways God's power would be displayed in the future. He could not have anticipated the plagues, the Red Sea, the manna, or other momentous events, but he believed God would be with him. God's call continued to be vitally present in Moses' awareness. He never forgot his call. God sought out Moses, not the other way around. A demand, not a suggestion, was God's instruction to go forth and set the people free.

Reading and reflecting on the life of Moses, I soon realized that the issues and struggles I faced as a chaplain were like the ones faced by Moses. Over the next fifty-plus years, I gained numerous insights into Moses' work. Reading the scripture passages and reflecting on the song has helped me apply Moses' experiences to my own calling. These insights have often helped me to respond appropriately to varied situations.

Notes were jotted down and stuffed in a file. The correlation between Moses' experiences and my life became clearer. Occasionally, I would scribble down some ideas. Sometimes, I experimented with an outline. After retiring, I began to give serious consideration to sharing these ideas. I think of this work as a way to give back in gratitude for the joy I have experienced as a chaplain.

I was privileged to serve in seven different organizations with widely differing environments. I have served in a suburban general hospital, a large state mental hospital, a youthful offender prison, a close security prison, a progressive mental health institute, the US Army Reserve (including a prisoner of war camp in Saudi Arabia), and a hospice. Despite large differences in these environments, the basic principles I learned from Moses have been applicable to all them. I believe that the study and application of these principles can be helpful to chaplains serving in their specific settings.

Moses served in a variety of roles. These included lawgiver, counselor, advocate with pharaoh, organizer, guide in the desert, disciplinarian, interpreter of God's message, and others.

Chaplains work in unique settings and may often be misunderstood or ignored by other ministers. The recipients of a chaplain's ministry sometimes ask, "Are you a real minister?" Church members, coworkers, and volunteers make sweeping assumptions about the value of their chaplains. Even many supervisors have difficulty conceptualizing the value of their chaplain. These misunderstandings emphasize the critical necessity of clear and comprehensive guidance for chaplains. I hope this book will facilitate that effort.

Many Christians assume that chaplain ministry is simply an extension of the pastoral ministry of a church. There are numerous similarities; there are also important differences that affect how a chaplain approaches the ministry. Four differences are unity, beliefs, programming, and supervision.

Unity

Unity is that sense of belonging that comes from common elements in the life of participants. Spiritual disciplines and activities are meaningful when there is a sense of togetherness. We say that we "belong" to a certain congregation or faith.

Unity emerges when the group has things in common. A church has history, traditions, expectations, and other unifying elements they share. Chaplains serve in environments where unity nearly always comes from something else. All are prisoners, all are military persons, all are patients, or all have some other characteristic in common.

Community church members usually worship in family groups. Sometimes, three and four generations of families attend the same church at the same time. Often, a history of participation goes back many years. A high degree of commitment results in a sense of permanence. Family groups foster a diversity of ages in the church. Social, economic, and educational similarities are common.

Chapel participants display a quite different pattern. Generally, participants in chapel programs are not considered members, though some refer to the chapel as their church. Individuals make up the majority of participants. Family members may be welcomed, but few attend. While many participants are similar in age groups, their ethnicity may have much diversity.

Short-term ministry becomes the norm in most settings. Even long-term prisons have a bigger turnover than would be expected. Some settings have such rapid turnover that it is unrealistic for the chaplain to expect more than one or two visits with an individual. Chapel participants have not been worshipping together for long periods of time.

Traditions are few, if any. Many participants in chapel activities do not know each other. Group type elements in worship may contribute to a sense of unity. Such things as unison readings, prayer requests, and greeting each other are examples.

Beliefs

Theology is a common thread in churches. Many church members treasure their beliefs to the point that they will defend their beliefs to anyone who disagrees with them. Chaplains minister to a congregation with widely differing views. Some participants in chapel services object when beliefs expressed do not concur with their own. Others are encouraged when they witness diversity in fellowship. Similarities and differences can easily surface when talking with a person of another faith perspective. Visiting a devout Jewish man in the hospital where I was pursuing my internship, I learned a great lesson. I told him I was a Christian student chaplain and I was not sure what to talk about with a Jewish person. This kindly, elderly gentleman said, "Why don't we start with what we have in common." Recalling his advice worked well for me many times when talking with persons with obviously different beliefs.

Programming

Planning and organizing of church activities is a cooperative effort. Church members have input or choices into what subjects or methods are included in church life. Most chaplains find that the programming of ministry functions falls entirely to them. This can be a mixed bag. A certain consistency comes when one person plans the emphases and the activities. Blind spots can also occur, and important issues may be overlooked. Suggestions from the people served and from staff and volunteers should be respected even if not implemented.

A pastoral services advisory board in one hospital gave opportunities to evaluate ministries. The members met twice a year to review past and future efforts. I felt a sense of support from the group.

Supervision

I have heard "everybody has a supervisor of some kind." Some faith groups have a hierarchical system where bishops, elders, deacons, overseers, or other such persons provide supervision. Other groups emphasize congregational authority where major decisions are approved by the congregation. Whether there is congregational or hierarchical leadership, the goals and purposes in a church are largely the same, and consensus is usually achieved.

Chaplains have supervision from at least two directions, ecclesiastical and bureaucratic. An endorsing organization from the chaplain's own faith perspective is responsible to provide broad guidance for nurture and oversight for each chaplain. Rarely does an endorsing body get directly involved in a chaplain's ministry, and when it does, it is often due to a controversial issue. Day-to-day supervision comes in many forms. Where there are multiple chaplains, one chaplain will be senior. The senior chaplain will be supervised by someone else.

Some chaplains have expressed the frustration of being supervised by someone who does not identify with his or her spiritual values. Supervisors may take a variety of approaches. Some would rather not be bothered. The opposite of this might be the supervisor who wants to see the chaplain in the image of some beloved former pastor. Chaplains can expect their supervisor to have different theological positions which can be minor or radical. Looking for similarities with respect can build bridges of understanding.

My purpose for this book is to convey the deep significance of Moses' example for chaplains. Three groups form the primary audience for this book.

The first group of people are those considering going into chaplaincy. They need to be informed about the potential challenges they may face. I will also suggest some possible ways to confront challenges and take advantage of opportunities.

Second, current chaplains may also enhance some skills and insights while gaining perspective. Perspective has to do with the location where you see *from*. Consider watching a football game. Sitting on the fifty-yard line, you can get a fairly clear picture of midfield where most of the game is played, but you will find it nearly impossible to measure movement near the goal line. On the other hand, if you sit near the end zone, you can't see the action at midfield or at the opposite end; however, you can have a clear view of field goal attempts. We cannot be at all these places at once (except when watching on TV). A chaplain cannot see all parts of an issue, event, or conflict. Patience, reflection, and consultation with peers enable a chaplain to have a viewpoint that is fair and accurate.

Those who work with chaplains make up the third group. Administrators of institutions, denominational officials, pastors, military superiors, and seminary professors may gain broader understanding of chaplains' ministry. This, in turn, may lead to more effective teamwork with chaplains.

Readers may get the impression that chaplaincy is all about difficulties. This is definitely not the case. There are many heartwarming memories. Early one morning, driving home after taking a friend to the airport, a motorcycle came up beside my car. When the rider waved, I realized it must be someone who knew me. He raised the visor of his helmet when we stopped at a traffic light. I recognized him as a former inmate who had been a member of a drug treatment group and who had attended chapel services. He immediately pulled up his sleeve to show me he had no needle tracks on his arms. There are more blessings than difficulties in the ministry of chaplains. Blessings are joyful and make the ministry meaningful. Difficulties need careful scrutiny to avoid overreacting which can result in reducing effectiveness of ministry.

Much is said in this book about Moses, but it is not a book about Moses. I have shared some experiences of other chaplains I have known or worked with, but this is not a book about them. My own experiences are included, but it is not a book about me. I want this book first, last, and always to be a book about God. I want to convince readers that God works through chaplains. I want readers to see that God works with chaplains today as much as with Moses. I hope reading this book will help my readers in three ways.

1. To gain insights into what to expect.
2. To gain confidence that God will walk with you.
3. To gain skills and abilities to respond to situations that arise.

I am writing from my perspective of Christianity. I have endeavored to write in a broad enough style that people of other faith groups may find these lessons helpful. My assumption is that my readers will have at least an overall familiarity with the biblical accounts about Moses. I hope my readers will benefit from my experience. I am convinced God called me to this ministry and that it was the best thing I could ever have done.

CHAPTER 1

Moses Was a Chaplain

Why call Moses a chaplain? By definition, a chaplain is a minister to people in unusual circumstances. Usually, this means being away from home. Residing in a prison, hospital, or other facility leads to a heightened awareness of being away from home. Home seems very far away even when the actual distance is small. The sights, sounds, and smells of a hospital add to this feeling. Restrictions of a prison have the same effect. Military persons may feel far from home especially on "unaccompanied tours." People may be away from home for many reasons. Some are honorable, as in military service. Some are shameful, as in a prison sentence. Some are due to physical or mental difficulties. Whatever the reason, people away from home require the ministry of chaplains. People away from home need the same things they get from their home congregation. These include worship, spiritual connection, Bible study, fellowship, rituals, crisis ministry, opportunities for service, pastoral care, and counseling. Through these activities, a chaplain can offer participants some powerful values which may include encouragement, hope, purpose, forgiveness, and others. Efforts should be made to provide all these if possible. Activities will not be provided in the same proportions as a local church. For example, a chaplain is likely to be involved in less fellowship activities and more crisis ministry.

Being away from home precipitates some needs. Separation requires changes for family members left at home. These include the practical matters of managing finances, supervising children, managing time, living arrangements, and nurturing relationships through communication. Emotional issues usually complicate relationships in a family. Anger, depression, anxiety, fear, loneliness, and other painful feelings—combined with practical matters—can make life miserable for families. Chaplains must be aware of these dynamics and address them in preaching, counseling groups, Bible study, and in pastoral counseling.

Egypt was not home for the Israelite people even though they had lived there all their lives. The sons of Israel came to Egypt to get food during a famine. Joseph invited them to bring their father and move to Egypt. Beginning with about seventy adults, their number increased to over six hundred thousand during the next 230 years. They were there for many generations. Joseph was in good favor with pharaoh because of his prediction of fat years and lean years. Later, a new pharaoh came to power who did not know Joseph, and things changed drastically (Exodus 1:8).

Pharaoh now feared that the large number of Israelites might rebel against him. He tried to limit the growth of the Israelite population by ordering the midwives to kill all Israelite baby boys (Exodus 1:16). Pharaoh enslaved them and treated them with brutality.

> They made their lives bitter with
> hard labor in brick and mortar and with
> all kinds of work in the fields; in all their
> hard labor the Egyptians used them ruth-
> lessly. (Exodus 1:14)

Stories of their homeland were passed down for many generations, repeated, and treasured. They dreamed of a promised land of "milk and honey" (Exodus 13:5).

The Israelites were away from a home they had never known. They needed a chaplain to minister to them. Moses was their chaplain.

The Significance of Moses

I referred to Moses as my hero in the introduction. *Webster's Dictionary* gives the following definition of *hero*.

> A man of distinguished courage or
> ability, admired for his brave deeds and

noble qualities…or has performed a heroic
act and is regarded as a model or ideal.[2]

Moses fulfills this definition so completely that the
dictionary could have just included a picture of Moses if
one existed.

The three largest faith groups in the world express
high esteem for Moses and his teachings. They are Islam,
Judaism, and Christianity. Moses has been honored in
Scripture. His name is mentioned 737 times in the Old
Testament. The 80 times he is mentioned in the New
Testament is more than any other Old Testament person.
His significance is found throughout the Bible. The book
of Hebrews portrays Moses' significance as one of the people held up as examples of faith (Hebrews 11:23–29). The
writer of the book of Hebrews sought to inspire Christians
by describing how faith was implemented different ways by
their ancestors. The list included Moses.

> By faith Moses, when he had grown
> up, refused to be known as the son of
> Pharaoh's daughter. He chose to be mis-
> treated along with the people of God
> rather than to enjoy the pleasures of sin
> for a short time. (Hebrews 11:24–26)

Jesus demonstrated the significance of Moses in the
transfiguration experience. Peter James and John saw Moses
pictured with Elijah and Jesus. The dramatic event shocked

them to the point that they fell to the ground awestruck. Matthew, Mark, and Luke recorded this event.

> Jesus took Peter, John and James with him and went up onto a mountain to pray. As he was praying, the appearance of his face changed, and his clothes became as bright as a flash of lightning. Two men, Moses and Elijah, appeared in glorious splendor, talking with Jesus. (Luke 9:28–31)

Moses' words were important to Jewish Christians and Gentile Christians in the first-century church.

> For Moses has been preached in every city from the earliest times and is read in the synagogues on every Sabbath. (Acts 15:21)

Near the end of Moses' life, God showed his approval.

> I will do the very thing you have asked, because I am pleased with you and I know you by name. (Exodus 33:17)

Moses is mentioned more than one hundred times in the Qur'an. Chapter Surah 33:69 states that Moses was "honorable in God's sight."[3] *Life Magazine* published an entire issue entitled "Moses—How His Teachings Shaped the World." The following appears in the introduction:

> Moses remains one of the most influential figures of all time…and as a story of hope and liberation, the narrative of Moses has deeply influenced people and religions all over the world—not least on American soil: The Pilgrims who came here seeking religious freedom, the Founding Fathers of the United States, and the African Americans who sought freedom from slavery all took their cues from Moses. To this day, images of the prophet in US government buildings—including the Capitol, the Library of Congress, and the Supreme Court—reflect the influence of his law-giving legacy on the country.[4]

Chaplains in many settings today are significant members of the team. Some coworkers do not recognize the chaplain's significance, but generally, the more seasoned colleagues do. From their experience, they value the chaplain's ministry.

A high-ranking official at the facility where I worked came to share with me. His son was seriously injured in an automobile accident and taken to the nearby trauma center. He told me the night shift chaplain stopped by the waiting room frequently throughout the night. He sat with the family, prayed with the family, and simply listened as the family wept and shared. This official made it a point to tell me how good it was to have a chaplain present in their time of need. He said he looked forward to each time the chaplain came by on his rounds.

My younger daughter served as a registered nurse in an infant intensive care unit. The babies were quite young and quite sick. Many did not survive. At times, it became clear the child would not survive and would have to be taken off life support. A nurse and a chaplain would always be present as a parent held the child and watched the machines being taken away. Having been part of this process a number of times, my daughter told me how comforting it was to both the family and to her to have a chaplain present.

Great significance attaches to these kinds of events. Recipients of this ministry remember it for many years. Chaplains often remember these kinds of events with gratification. Less noticeable events often lead the chaplain to a sense of fulfillment. I was present when a group of mental health professionals dealt with a young man on an out-of-control rampage. After he was restrained, I sat with him offering comforting words as he continued to struggle. Eventually, he calmed down. My supervisor mentioned this incident on my next employee evaluation. I found this almost humorous because on the same day, I sat on the floor with a man crouched in a corner quietly sobbing. I felt the latter incident was just as significant as the more dramatic one. Chaplains must recognize for themselves the significance of the unrecognized day-to-day encounters.

CHAPTER 2

Moses Had to Know Who He Was

Everyone faces the developmental task of forming an identity. "Who am I? What is my purpose in life? What is life all about?" Questions like these are encountered in adolescence but also continue for our entire life. The questions keep coming back to be refined and redefined, sometimes consciously, sometimes not. Experiencing a changing life situation—such as marriage, divorce, career change, births, or deaths—often raise questions of identity. Sometimes, questions emerge again for no apparent reason.

Our identity as a chaplain is important. We must strive to develop our self-concept. A clear picture of who we are will help us empathize with the needs of others. A psychiatrist at the Menninger Clinic once told an audience, including chaplains, "You cannot understand others until you understand yourself."[5]

Two primary factors contribute to our identity as a chaplain. First, the history and influence of family provides a foundation for understanding oneself. Second, for chaplains, the call of God instructs this critical area of consideration. I have heard that a minister's identity is more about who he or she *is* than what he or she *does*.

Moses had to work out his identity. It wasn't easy. Three major cultural and religious groups influenced Moses' self-concept. They were the Egyptians, the Israelites, and Jethro, a Midianite priest. The symbols of belonging and of identity were confusing and contradictory. He was born an Israelite but given an Egyptian name. Adopted by his Egyptian stepmother, he was nursed and nurtured by his birth mother and born a slave without social or legal standing.

He had opportunities and an education. His people were subject to the unlimited power of pharaoh, but he was given privileges. Scriptures do not give us much information about Moses' stepmother. Josephus gives the following description of the child Moses. He reports that the Egyptian princess (called Batyah or Thermuthis) adopted him so that he could become pharaoh after her father. At least one movie depicted the scenario of Moses being groomed to be pharaoh. Josephus tells that she had no son of her own but found Moses to be beautiful. When three years of age, she referred to him as tall. Moses beauty was so remarkable that when people saw him on the road, they would stand and look at him for a long time. His understanding and quick apprehension was superior to others the same age. Moses stepmother took the small child to her father. While holding Moses in his arms and hugging him, he put his crown on the child. Moses threw the crown on the ground. Some saw it as an omen and wanted to kill Moses because of the perceived insult, but pharaoh refused.[6]

Moses became schooled in the Egyptian educational system. Phillip Swanson described a rigorous schedule which began at about age four. Strict discipline was enforced. Subjects included reading, writing, mathematics, and sciences. All areas of learning included magic and superstition except mathematics. Ethics and good manners were highly valued. Though trained as an Egyptian, he was not given any title or position that we know of.

Egyptian religion was a mixture of seemingly random concepts. Moses would have been familiar with them. Monotheism was encouraged when Pharaoh Akhenaton proclaimed Aten as the "only god unique and supreme over all the universe." Akhenaton died before Moses' birth, and this belief faded. Some monotheistic influence remained. Egyptian priests were very powerful. Any concept of sin was absent. Animals were venerated, especially the hawk. The gods were considered immoral and were to be feared. Astronomy played a big part in their religion.[7]

The Israelites were a proud people with a rich history going back to Abraham. Now the Egyptians enslaved them and forced them into hard work. Brutality and disrespect were their daily fare. They worshiped the God of Abraham, Isaac, and Jacob. Priests were active in the community, and sacrifices were offered. They formed twelve tribes named after the twelve sons of Jacob (Israel), thus the name "children of Israel." Levites were one of the tribes. Levi was the son of Leah, Jacob's least favorite wife. Leah's animosity may have carried over to her sons Simeon and Levi. Levites had the reputation of being "men of wrath and urgency." Years earlier, an entire town was slaughtered because of an injustice done to their sister Dinah (Genesis 34:1–2, 25–26). Jacob condemned this act and ordered that the Levites not be given land but spread out among the other tribes so that their wrath would be diffused (Genesis 34, 49). The Levites were given responsibility to take care of the tent of meeting. They became priests.

Family members and others connected with Moses and assisted in his growth, development, and preparation. Miriam, his sister, literally watched over Moses from birth throughout his life. Aaron, his older brother, was intimately involved in Moses' ministry. Like most brothers, they had disagreements and conflicts. Some of them were severe. Not much is known about Moses' parents, but we can assume that they kept informed about his life. They likely gave him much information regarding the history and values of his people.

Moses sided with the plight of the slaves to the point that he killed an Egyptian when he saw him beating an Israelite. Perhaps, Moses thought he could gain acceptance from the Israelites by killing the man who was mistreating them. If the Israelites appreciated this, they did not show it. In fact, the deed was widely known but not with respect (Exodus 2:11–14).

Moses fled from pharaoh and Egypt. He stopped at a well in Midian. Some shepherds and two young women were watering their flocks. The two young women were the daughters of a priest of Midian named Jethro. The shepherds chased the women away so they could water their flocks first. Moses kept the shepherds away, and he watered their flock. Jethro's daughters recognized Moses as an Egyptian and told their father what happened. Jethro took Moses into his family and became like the father he apparently never knew. Moses now had some people of similar Semitic heritage that he could connect to with strong attachment (Exodus 2:15–22).

Jethro, a descendant of Midian, was a son of Abraham by his second wife Keturah. Jethro was a priest and worshipped the God of Abraham, Isaac, and Jacob. The Israelites and the Midianites both traced their ancestry back to Abraham, so in a distant way, they were relatives. Moses knew he was an Israelite, but he did not quite fit into either the Israelite or Egyptian world.

The identity process continued in the "quiet years" he spent with the Midianites. The scriptures offer few details about this forty-year period. A lot happened that affected his concept of self. He was now living in an environment somewhere between the vastly different worlds of the Israelites and the Egyptians. He was not subject to the control of others as his people were. He could come and go as he wished. On the other hand, life as a wandering shepherd was probably hard. Food, water, and protection could not be taken for granted but must be sought with much effort. He learned to live from day to day.

Meanwhile, Moses also raised a family. Moses married Zipporah, Jethro's daughter, and they had two sons, Gershom and Eliezer (Exodus 3:21, 18:3–4).

Moses' father-in-law had a profound influence on him. At last, here is someone who accepted him gladly without suspicion or conditions. Jethro was a prominent and respected person. As a leader of the Midianites, he taught Moses spiritual and practical insights and many crucial skills needed in years to come. Jethro continued to encourage Moses. When he announced his call from God and his intention to return to Egypt, Jethro blessed him (Exodus 4:18–20). After Moses' departure, Jethro saw him at least seven more times.[8]

Moses initially took his wife and sons with him to Egypt (Exodus 4:20). At some point, Moses sent his family to Jethro, perhaps for safety. Jethro brought Moses' family to him a few months after the people left Egypt. When Moses met Jethro, they greeted each other with a ceremonial kiss. Clearly, Moses had a strong affectionate bond with his father-in-law (Exodus 18:5–7). Jethro's influence most likely laid the foundation of Moses' concept of God. In the midst of these conflicting influences in his history, how could Moses determine who he was? It came together for him when God called him. The influence of his life experiences and of his call from God at the burning bush had powerful effects. His family was in contact through his early years, so Moses surely knew the events around his birth. He was aware of his relatives and their mounting struggles. Perhaps, he was acquainted with Israelite leaders and friends in the community. Their lifestyles, beliefs, and practices would contribute to Moses' understanding of himself.

Moses' dramatic call from God was powerful and life changing. Prior to his call, Moses seemed to be more concerned with the past than with the future. His priority was himself and his own safety. After his call, Moses seemed to be more concerned with the future than the past. His priorities now were the Israelites and their well-being.

He never seemed to doubt his purpose after the burning bush. An important part of this experience was learning God's name. Names were considered highly significant. Knowing God's name produced a special relationship with God. More about God's name will be covered in chapter 3.

A chaplain's sense of a call from God can be an important facet of a chaplain's identity. This sense of being called to a purpose can reinforce the work of a chaplain. Awareness of an intimate relationship with God can motivate and energize a chaplain.

Many and varied are the forms that a call can take when coming to a person. Isaiah, Paul, and Moses received their call with dramatic events. These dramatic experiences left no doubt in their minds that God chose them for specific purposes. God's call does not need to be dramatic. James and John were practicing their ordinary profession of fishing when Jesus came to them and offered them a choice. They quickly committed to becoming a disciple.

God's call in modern times may not be dramatic or clear, but it is an important part of a chaplain's identity. A gradual awareness of a person's abilities, a conviction regarding the needs, feedback from friends and family, or perhaps a restlessness may contribute to an emerging sense of call. Unrealistic expectations of some dramatic event may produce confusion and delay the process of clarifying the call.

My own call to ministry, a gradual process, included much uncertainty, confusion, and misgivings. At the time, I was married with two children (two more came along before I graduated seminary). My wife and I struggled together trying to decide if God was calling. I had a good job at a major airline, and we owned a home. We had extended family and many friends nearby. The future looked bright for us, but something about our lives did not feel right. I was restless, feeling like I was missing something. We were actively involved in church and a fellowship of young couples.

Meaning and purpose came from our participation in church. That led to increased activity. Increased activity led to even more meaning and purpose. From time to time, I wondered if there was something more that God wanted for me. My wife and I talked and prayed about it often but could not find a clear direction. Was God calling me (us) to ministry? My only image of a minister was either a pastor or a minister of music. I had no skills in either arena—I really didn't. The whole idea seemed completely unrealistic. Nevertheless, the feelings persisted. The inclination became stronger and stronger. I started taking college classes at night, thinking that if God was calling, I had better get started on an education. If God was not calling, getting a degree would still be a good idea. Heavy demands from my employer and rotating shifts interrupted the classes, making it difficult to continue. After three years, I had only completed one year of college work.

We realized that we were going to be forced to make a decision. I could not have it both ways. If I continued my part-time education, a very long period of time would be required. If I decided to go to school full time, I would have to resign my job and lose the needed income. I didn't know what to do. An honest evaluation of my gifts reinforced the belief that I was not cut out to be a preacher or musician. Still the feeling persisted and became even stronger.

Finally, we sold the house, resigned our jobs, and moved away to college. I now felt that God would some-how reveal to me the direction I should go.

A small rural part-time church called me to be their pastor while a college student. With considerable anxiety, I gave it a try. Maybe I could learn to be a pastor. The loving people in the church gave me and my family more than we could give them. When we moved on to seminary, the people filled our freezer with produce from their farms.

Through the college years, we accumulated a consider-able amount of debt. We considered the possibility of stay-ing with the church after graduation and going to work in a nearby factory. This would allow us to pay down our debts, but it would also mean a delay in transitioning to seminary.

Then an amazing thing happened. The chairman of the Christianity department called me in and shocked me with a completely unexpected proposal. There was a fund from the estate of a lady who wanted to help ministerial stu-dents. I could receive a grant but only if I went ahead and enrolled in seminary. We moved to another state over eight hundred miles away from family and friends. It turned out that the grant was just enough to make the move and rent an apartment.

During seminary years, I served as pastor of another small rural part-time church in a depressed former coal mining area. Looking ahead, I expected to have a career as a mediocre pastor working hard to be adequate. Crisis situations came up more often than would have been expected in a small church. It seemed that people wanted to share their troubles with me. This was a signal that I did not recognize.

A breakthrough came in my very last semester in seminary. I took a course entitled "The Pastor's Hospital Ministry." The class met one day a week at a local hospital with the hospital chaplain teaching the course. I finally realized that the chaplaincy was where God was sending me, though I did not see it until late in my seminary studies. Now I could see that my temperament, understandings, and gifts would be needed for a chaplain. In retrospect, I can see God preparing me all along. I soon signed up for a year of clinical pastoral education (CPE). A discussion of CPE will be included in chapter 6.

Reflecting to a career of over fifty years, I am convinced that it was the right thing for me. I can also see that, throughout my career, God has put me in the right place at the right time. For example, ministering in the hospice setting while in my thirties would have been difficult. Conversely, serving the youthful offenders while in my sixties may not have been successful. Chaplains must periodically seek to evaluate and revise their sense of call as time and experiences dictate.

CHAPTER 3

Moses Had to Know Who God Was

Moses knew about the many different beliefs and practices in Egypt. They had many gods and many concepts of gods.

By contrast, the Israelites believed in the God of Abraham, Isaac, and Jacob. Their beliefs were connected to Abraham's relationship with God. Abraham's call to leave home and kinsmen informed their history. God promised that a great nation would descend from Abraham and would then bless "all the nations of the world" (Genesis 12:1–3, 18:18).

The Israelites had elders and priests. The history of Abraham, Isaac, and Jacob was passed along and preserved through oral traditions. Moses would have known the history. He never lost sight of the fact that it was God doing these things.

Two huge events stand out which influenced Moses' concept of God. The burning bush call and the giving of the law were the most dramatic events of his life. Both worked to give Moses a clear concept of God. God spoke to Moses directly in these events and other times as well. Seeing a bush burning without being consumed had to be a puzzling and fearful happening. God used this method to get Moses' attention. It worked. In this process, Moses was given the tremendous task of obtaining freedom for his people. Moses learned much about God, and he learned God's name, Yahweh. God's name was a crucial part of God's revelation.

In ancient times, a person's name included a powerful significance. More than just identification, a name included a sense of the essence of a person. Change in a person's life usually resulted in a new name. Jacob became Israel. Saul of Tarsus became Paul the apostle. Moses asked God for his name, and God supplied it. The name Yahweh or "I Am" motivated Moses and focused his understanding. This led to Moses' high level of dedication (Exodus 3:14).

Moses asked God for a sign to verify the call. Experiencing the rod turning into a snake was an immediate sign. Another sign seems curious. God told Moses that after the people were freed, they would worship on the same mountain (Exodus 3:12). Moses was likely confused since this sign could not be seen until after Moses' obedience. Chaplains often do not see the effects of ministry until later.

God gave the law to the people through Moses. The people needed guidance and structure. Though Moses' leadership was well established by this time, the revelation of the law and being in the very presence of God was a powerful event. Moses learned much and clarified much about God. His encounter with God changed Moses. So powerful was this encounter with God that when Moses returned, even his appearance changed. Moses needed to be transformed by God to be properly prepared for his mission. God changed Moses by revealing himself in a way compatible with Moses ability to hear. Continued refinement and transformation was required for success. God always provided this exposure and resulting transformation which cannot be done entirely on one's own.

God's revelation of himself is the key ingredient of Moses' understanding of who God is. God's revelation is important today as chaplains seek to know who God is and what God is calling and equipping them to do. Revelation rarely, if ever, comes in such a dramatic fashion as with Moses, but God's revelation instructs and enables us. We must grapple with such questions as, "Who is God? What is God like? What is God's claim on me? What is my relationship with God?" Chaplains can find God's revelation in many ways. These include at least the following. Studying scripture and other writings, realizing that scriptures can have many layers of meaning, openness to alternatives perhaps nontraditional meanings should be considered. Reflection on one's experiences and history can be helpful. An honest and perhaps courageous assessment of one's strengths and weaknesses may provide direction.

What seemingly coincidental things have come about? An example is my struggle with scheduling night school classes and my employer's demands. How can these events point us in the way God wants us to go? Listening to feedback from other people can be instructive since other people can see in us what we often cannot see in ourselves. Others may see strengths we are unaware of or growing edges we would prefer to ignore. Even people with whom we don't have a good relationship can give us feedback. As hard as it may be to hear, we must consider criticism from others.

Sergeant (name omitted) was my supervisor in the Air National Guard. I was a young enlisted person still in my teens. He was foulmouthed, harsh, and demanding. In his eyes, I could do nothing right. I did not like him, and he did not like me. He seemed to take every opportunity to criticize and berate me. My self-confidence took a beating. I mentally rejected everything he said but remembered much of it. Reflecting on it years later, I had to admit that the sergeant was right more than I had thought. Reflection upon his harsh words, some of it years later, helped me to accept my flaws and learn from them.

Assessment of one's skills and suitability is important. What are our strengths and weaknesses? What is our temperament? How do we communicate? Do our skills fit best in public or in private ministry? Responding to opportunities can help to clarify goals and objectives. As a young man in my early twenties and before I began to approach ministry, I explored several career choices. I liked my job repairing typewriters, but today, that field has virtually disappeared. A brief stint as *The Fuller Brush Man* convinced me a career in sales was not for me. I realized that an engineering career would not work for me. It seems that God was guiding me to where my gifts would lie, but I could not see it then. Ultimately, over time, I embraced my gifts and built on them. Often, we cannot see God's long-term goals until after the fact.

A personal encounter with God led Moses to a deeper personal relationship with God. Chaplains who nurture a close relationship with God seem to find fulfillment in ministry.

CHAPTER 4

Moses Communicated with God

M oses talked to God. He spoke openly. Moses expressed anger to God (Exodus 5:22). He told God about his anger toward the people (Exodus 17:4). Moses prayed to God about specific problems (Exodus 8:30). He asked God for guidance and got it (Exodus 15:25). God spoke to Moses at least sixty-six times in the book of Exodus.

> The Lord would speak to Moses face
> to face, as a man speaks with his friend.
> (Exodus 33:11)

Moses' close relationship with God led to effective communication. Moses took frustration, anger, and questions to God. He listened to God and moved with assurance after spending time with God.

I have never heard God speak in an audible voice as he did with Moses. I have not experienced dreams that showed me what to do as Joseph did before Jesus' birth. I have had times in which I believed God spoke to me, not in words but sometimes in subtle awareness, sometimes in personal thoughts, sometimes deep emotion, sometimes in ways I can't describe. The conviction of God's guidance produced direction. All this underscores the urgency of a meaningful prayer life for chaplains.

Prayer must be rightly understood and regularly practiced. Many concepts of prayer are put forward, so saying what prayer *is not* may be easier than saying *what prayer is*. Prayer is not a magic trick to make things happen. It is not casting a vote for what you want from God. It is not a way to make decisions. Prayer is open, honest sharing with God. Any emotion, question, fear, or confusion will be heard by God.

Personal prayer brings great benefits to a chaplain. Many books, classes, seminars, and retreats are available. Contemplative prayer and centering prayer have become popular modes of spiritual growth.

This chapter will focus on the use of prayer in chaplain ministry. Clients present a wide variety of concerns for prayer. Chaplains should try to discern concerns of the client and address them. We must try to see the need behind the statement if possible. We provided Bibles to inmates upon request. I generally took the men into the office where I said some things about the Bible. Then I would ask, "How is it going with you?" Often, this elicited responses like, "My wife is divorcing me." It is important to see the need behind the need.

A young unmarried patient in the mental hospital's long-term care unit said, "Please pray that I will get pregnant." I could not pray for that. I worked to see the need behind the need. I asked her about family, children, and motherhood. I used these values in the prayer. A lady in a hospice care center said, "Please pray that I will die today." I offered that prayer aloud in front of her.

A retired chaplain in a hospice care center with advanced dementia did not recognize me or his son or daughter. He served as a chaplain in World War II. Occasionally, a memory would surface which indicated a marvelous career. One day, I asked if we should have prayer. Instead of answering, he started praying. The beautiful words displayed a life of deep spirituality. He ministered to me.

A lady asked me to pray for her, a common occurrence. When I saw her again, she asked if I had prayed for her. My shame was evident when I confessed that I had forgotten. I promised myself that it would not happen again. I put some two-by-two-inch cards in my datebook. Whenever someone requested prayer, I would ask their concerns and wrote them on a card. An unexpected benefit was that the client seemed to know I was taking their requests seriously.

Hospice patients received home visits from a chaplain after a request. I assumed, since they requested a chaplain visit, they would want prayer. Most of them did. I began to notice that some were uncomfortable when I asked if they wanted prayer. A new tactic was implemented. I said something like, "I always pray for my patients. I can pray now or include you in my prayer later." Most of them wanted prayer at that time. Some were more comfortable with later.

Prayer is the most basic form of worship, both private and communal. Worship with mental patients was different from other settings but also quite meaningful to me. The absence of pretense produced authenticity. A lack of impulse control led to some surprises. Speaking out during the sermon was common. A patient might ask a question or disagree with something I said. God must be pleased with the spontaneity.

I devoted about one-third of the thirty-minute service to prayer. Several categories of prayer included thanksgiving, concerns, praise, and confession (silent). Twice as many thanks were mentioned than concerns. When most patients and staff complained about the quality of institutional food, one lady expressed thanks for the food. I later learned she spent most of her life in poverty, often going hungry.

A man always said, "I thank God for my life." He suffered a near fatal automobile crash which left him with permanent brain damage (his reason for admission).

Prayer can be a powerful resource for chaplains. Flexibility will help chaplains respond helpfully to the variety of ways prayer is practiced. A chaplain's role should include the use of prayer.

CHAPTER 5

Moses Had to Discover His Role

God gave Moses a call and a purpose. He did not give Moses exact details of how to accomplish it. Moses was responsible to figure it out. Moses could have tried to return to pharaoh's court to work from the inside for change. He might have gone to the Hebrews to be a priest, motivating the people. He was of the priestly tribe of Levi. He could have sought to be one of the Israelite elders, exercising control over the people. Instead, he went to Egypt without a title or authority except what God endowed him with. Moses' role developed from his call and his purpose. It developed gradually and seemed to change as needed throughout his life. Chaplains are often left to devise their own roles.

Someone pointed out that the most troubling line in any job description is the last line. It is the line that reads, "And other duties." Chaplains are expected to take on other duties which do not match with a spiritual role. While wanting to be helpful, chaplains should seek to guard the unique role of a chaplain.

Four foundational functions combined to form Moses' role. These can be seen as a combination of actions and ways of thinking. These also apply to chaplains today and should always be taken into account when considering one's role. They may also help to conceptualize a basic role for a chaplain.

1. Moses represented God. It was God's message that Moses delivered. It was God's commands that Moses enforced.
2. Moses represented his people. He spoke to Pharaoh on behalf of the people. He interceded with God on behalf of the people asking God not to destroy them (Exodus 32:30—32).
3. Moses ministered to the people. He loved them and wanted them to have a better life. He related to them as a group and also as individuals, Sometimes confronting large groups and at other times a single individual.
4. Moses provided leadership to the elders who had the responsibility to govern the people.

The same four foundational functions are crucial to chaplains today as they conceptualize their role.

1. A chaplain must maintain the conviction that he or she is representing God. This must be first, last, and always. It is God's message that the chaplain conveys. It is God's guidance that the chaplain must seek to follow. Often, others may think a chaplain represents primarily some organization such as the state, the military, a corporation, or a faith group. Regardless of what others may think, a chaplain must never lose sight of the connection with God.

2. Chaplains today represent a specific faith group. This is not a platform for narrowness or exclusiveness. It does not contradict the functions of number 1 above but compliments it. There can be a balance. This is a way of recognizing that the chaplain is not simply an individual doing his or her own thing but is a part of a network larger than himself or herself.

3. Ministering to the people is the most visible function of chaplaincy. Ministry will take different forms in different settings. Some forms of ministry will be covered in following chapters. A balance of ministry to individuals and groups should be sought. Ministry to staff and volunteers will produce good results. Many colleagues want to be helpful, but they can help best when they are nurtured by the chaplain. This requires leadership. Leadership requires establishing and promoting a vision which incorporates a direction to take and the necessary steps to pursue the vision. The

Israelite people knew they did not want to continue to be slaves, but they did not know exactly what they did want.

4. As situations changed, Moses actions had to change. When confronting pharaoh, Moses was unrelenting and uncompromising. When leading the people in the early stages of the exodus, Moses forcefully communicated his strong belief that God would carry them through. When receiving the law, Moses had to convince the people of the validity, importance, and relevance of the law.

During the years of wandering, the people needed structure that provided for their daily lives, their worship, and their sacrifices. Moses organized the people and gave them a tabernacle to meet this need. The people changed a lot during the forty years of wandering in the desert. When it was time for the people to enter the promised land, Moses prepared the people for the transition preparing the way for his successor, Joshua.

Chaplains today must be willing to tailor functions to fit a variety of settings. Ministry to prisoners with short-term sentences will be quite different from ministry to those with life sentences. Similarly, ministry to patients in community hospitals will be quite different from hospice patients. The Apostle Paul said, "I am all things to all people, so that I might win some" (1 Corinthians 9:22).

Building on the four foundational functions, a chaplain can develop a realistic role. From here, a chaplain must move on to specifics adapted to the organization where the chaplain serves. Here are a few settings where chaplains serve.

Military chaplains were established as an integral part of the army on July 29, 1775.[9] I once had a print of a painting depicting a chaplain leading a worship service when General George Washington was worshiping with his troops. Since then, military chaplains have gone through many transitions. At one time, they were civilians who volunteered to be with the troops short or long term. At another time, the commander of a unit often served as chaplain. It was not clear what rank a chaplain should be; therefore, a special rank of "chaplain" was instituted for a time which was approximately equal to the status of a captain.

The US Army produced documents to specify and clarify requirements, supervision, administrative functions, and role expectations. Army regulation 165-1 is the basic document, but there are also field manuals and pamphlets. These are admirable attempts to cover the wide variety of religious perspectives and environments while seeking a fair and balanced approach. While no document could cover every conceivable situation, I think they are helpful in avoiding misunderstanding.[10]

Military chaplains must be aware of some distinct characteristics not generally seen in other chaplain settings. Failure to take these into account can lower the military chaplain's effectiveness and result in frustration. These characteristics form much of the uniqueness of the military chaplain's role. A contribution to the military chaplain's role is an agreement between most of the nations in the world.

The Geneva Convention of 1949 specifies that all chaplains are to be classified as noncombatants. This means that chaplains may never take up a weapon in combat. Taking up a weapon makes a chaplain subject to disciplinary action.

The Geneva Convention states that upon capture, a chaplain should have access to the detention facility in order to minister to other prisoners. Military chaplains never exercise any command functions. They do not give orders or make tactical decisions. Even the head of the chaplains' school is a commandant, not a commander. Directives can be given within the sphere of a chaplain's role. When orders involving emergency situations or other important matters are needed, the chaplain must coordinate with someone in the chain of command.

Rank structure can be a mixed bag, sometimes resulting in confusion or barriers to ministry. Chaplain ranks range from first lieutenant (O-2) to major general (O-8). The majority of army chaplains hold the rank of captain or major. Privates can be intimidated when talking to a chaplain who is a major or lieutenant colonel. Higher ranked individuals may also feel some discomfort sharing with a chaplain of a lower rank. I have attempted to neutralize this barrier by conveying a concept that I learned in the US Army Chaplain Basic Course. The concept is that in a counseling or pastoral care situation, the chaplain is perceived as the same rank as the client. This approach has worked for me in many cases but not always. Attempting to encourage troops to contact the chaplain when needed, I often shared this concept with in-processing troops. I do not think this concept is an official part of the instruction. I remember that the instructor said it came from the British Army. Efforts to confirm this have been unsuccessful. Some chaplains lead worship services wearing robes or civilian clothes to minimize the differences in rank. The standard Protestant chaplain kit includes a black stole which covers the rank insignia when worn over the uniform.

Rank structure is important and gives chaplains access to information and people who can affect the ministry. Rank for chaplains is primarily for purposes of pay, assignments, and promotions. Army regulations present the role of a chaplain as more noteworthy than rank. This official doctrine is true for chaplains only. The proper address for me is Chaplain (COL) Kenneth W. Cook.[11]

Chaplains want everyone to share comfortably, especially with sensitive personal information. Army regulations spell out the availability and limits of confidentiality. Chaplains should ensure that they are fully cognizant of the provisions in order to communicate them to clients when needed.

Military courtesy and discipline help to build respect for the chaplain. Saluting and returning salutes is a time-honored demonstration of respect. First names are generally not used in conversations. Often, the title "chaplain" is used as a first name. I could never count the times I have heard, "Hey, Chaplain."

Participating in training exercises such as physical training or marching in the rain, mud, and cold can help the troops know that the chaplain is one of them. Firing a rifle is not required, but I usually tried to do it with the troops (though the scores were never recorded).

Prison chaplaincy shares some characteristics with military settings. The rank structure provides an understanding of lines of authority. Uniforms with the insignias of rank are worn by security staff. Prison personnel and activities generally fall into two broad categories, security, and treatment. Safety is a primary goal of security staff. Security takes priority over all else and, if necessary, preempts treatment staff activities. Treatment areas include education, counseling, medical, vocational training, and chaplaincy. Ideally, the security and treatment staffs work in harmony, each supporting the work of the other. It does not always work out that way. Each group may feel that the other is interfering with their area of responsibility.

A chaplain must seek to understand the priorities of the security staff and communicate that understanding to build a relationship of trust. Occasionally, the security staff at a prison where I worked would suspect that contraband was smuggled in through the chapel. Searches would be done which curtailed some chapel activities for an hour or two. In eleven years of prison ministry, only two items of contraband were ever found in the chapel. I was the one who found both of them. I think this encouraged the security staff to trust me. It was one thing to be a little less concerned about.

I always strived to be conscious of security issues. I think this perspective helped build good working relationships. I think the security staff was more comfortable knowing I was sensitive to security needs. Chaplains often find themselves in a middle ground between treatment and security. Chapter 7 will address this issue.

Medical facilities vary widely. Some are public, some are private, some are faith based, some are nonprofit, some are for profit, some are large, some are small, some are teaching hospitals, some are specialized, some are primarily inpatient, and others offer outpatient treatment. The differences can go on and on and have much to do with the chaplain's role. Common factors emerge in most medical facilities.

There will be more needs than a chaplain can ever meet. Developing a network of pastors, students, and other volunteers may enhance coverage. Chapter 13 will consider volunteer opportunities. Priorities will be hard to manage. Health care chaplains must make painful choices. Medical and administrative staff are often overloaded and stressed. Sensitivity toward staff is an important priority. When staff are rushing from one thing to another, family members may feel lost or abandoned. The presence of a chaplain who simply listens without judgment can ease the anxiety of families.

Spiritual support is always important. When offering spiritual support, a chaplain must be careful not to press one's own concepts. Making assumptions can cause a chaplain to miss important needs. For example, the birth of a child is usually a joyous time; however, if the birth triggers sadness, this signals issues of importance. Many other settings provide opportunities for meaningful chaplain ministry. Opportunities include nursing homes, rehab facilities, youth centers, assisted living facilities, veteran's programs, mental health centers, hospices, substance abuse recovery programs, industrial sites, shopping centers, and even the Atlanta Airport. Each of these unique settings present challenges when developing the role of the chaplain. Consultation, reflection, prayer, and attention to the four foundational functions can enable a chaplain to move through the many possibilities to arrive at an appropriate role for his or her unique setting.

As team members, chaplains serve important functions. Chaplains seek to interpret the client's spiritual issues to the staff. This can make treatment and diagnosis more effective. A seventy-year-old man came to the mental hospital where I worked with what was later determined to be a reaction to a combination of medicines he took. Asking many questions about the food and ingredients, a staff member described him as paranoid about food. When I talked with the gentleman, I learned that he was a longtime member of a faith group that encourages a vegetarian diet. This man had not eaten meat in many years, if ever. With this understanding, the staff began to look elsewhere for the cause of his problem. A chaplain I knew told me about this incident. A soldier in a combat zone came to him and told him about a sensitive personal need in his family. He needed to go home to resolve the issue. Unfortunately, the nature of the problem did not fit the guidelines of the regulations. The chaplain (a major) went to the soldier's company commander (a captain) and said, "This soldier needs to go home for a few days, but I cannot tell you why." Though somewhat reluctant, the commander approved it primarily because he knew the chaplain and trusted his judgment.

A clear and consistent concept of his or her role will enable a chaplain to function effectively. A senior chaplain told a group of military chaplains that they should meet with a new commander soon after assignment. The idea was to ask what the commander thought the chaplain's role should be. This is risky. Assuming that the commander is not trained in theology or pastoral care, he might name some inappropriate things. One chaplain was given the task of producing a newsletter, another was told to locate movies to show troops, and another was assigned to operate a bulldozer in a POW camp. I typically met with a new commander to explain my understanding of the chaplain's role. I took with me a typed sheet called "The Chaplain's Religious Activities Plan." I found all my commanders appreciative and almost always received good cooperation. Most chaplains are willing to step outside their role if needed, especially temporarily, but the primary emphasis must always refer to the basic role. In order to fulfill the demands of a chaplain's role, careful attention should be given to qualifications.

CHAPTER 6

Moses Did Not Feel Qualified

M oses had some serious disqualifications. They were not imagined or exaggerated. They were not excuses used to avoid responding to God's call.

The real and important hindrances would make the work more difficult. Nevertheless, God called Moses to free the Israelite people. God did not ask Moses to volunteer but ordered Moses to the task. Moses had a speech impediment. He knew speaking with clarity would convey a sense of authority. He needed to convey that authority to pharaoh and to the Israelite people. Moses told God that he was "not eloquent" but "slow of speech and tongue" (Exodus 4:10). God did not deny the handicap but compensated for it by appointing Aaron, Moses' older brother, to be spokesman.

A young Christian named Stephen was brought before the high priest on false charges (Acts 6–7). Defending against the charges, he gave a review of Israelite history. He described Moses as "powerful in speech and action." Does this mean that perhaps Moses learned to speak without the impediment? When confronting pharaoh and predicting the first few plagues, it was Aaron doing the talking. Later, it seems that Moses is doing the talking. Many chaplains have developed needed skills when they did not think they could.

I always knew I could not be a dynamic preacher. Efforts to be forceful in preaching came across as phony to me and probably to others. That realization disappointed me in the early days of ministry. I learned something that encouraged me. I evolved into a conversational style. I thought of this style as speaking to one person. After first seeing this as a shortcoming, I learned its value in a surprising way. While on Army Reserve duty in New York, I attended a worship service at Marble Collegiate Church. The pastor was the well-known author and speaker Norman Vincent Peale. When he spoke to the full auditorium, he stepped aside from the pulpit, folded his hands in front of him, and spoke in a soft, calm voice.

I don't remember a single word he said. What I do remember is the effectiveness of his style of communicating. Reflecting on that experience, I no longer minimized my style. Instead, I sought to develop and affirm it.

Moses feared that he could not have credibility with the Israelites. He had been away from Egypt for a long time. He was out of touch with current events in the Egyptian culture, as well as the Israelite camp. When he left Egypt forty years prior, he was a fugitive, having gotten into disfavor with both Egyptians and Israelites. Our mistakes of the past can certainly follow us but do not have to defeat us.

I once knew a chaplain who was competent, dedicated, and well prepared for a certain supervisory position in the Army Reserve. He wanted the position and would have been a wise choice. When the position became available, he was not selected and was transferred to another position in another state, much to his surprise and that of the other chaplains. He later found out that an impulsive remark he had made years earlier had stuck in the general's memory and he was passed over. Arguing the fairness or wisdom of the general's decision would be pointless. The lesson is that things from years past can come into play in the present.

Moses had qualifications that he likely was not aware of. He recognized his need for God's guidance. He was honest with God. Moses loved his people. He listened to advice from others but made his own decisions. Moses learned valuable skills for desert survival. God chose Moses because of his potential to learn and do the will of God.

Moses' past experiences gave him understandings that he could not have gotten otherwise. Painful experiences taught Moses much. Shepherding for Jethro was radically different from Moses' life before fleeing from pharaoh.

Charles Swindoll lists three things Moses learned in the desert. They are the development of a servant's attitude, the willingness to be obscure, and the ability to rest and rely on God.[12] The sheep were oddly similar to the Israelites Moses would later lead. Sheep do not understand human instructions but instinctively follow a shepherd they trust. Sheep are unable to decide things for themselves. Instead, they wander off, get lost, and get hurt. The Israelites followed Moses because they trusted him in the important matters even though they complained and wanted to rebel. Moses' personality characteristics came into play. Loyalty, faithfulness, caring, uncompromising, and sacrifice worked to maintain his credibility.

Moses may have felt he would be rejected again by the Israelites. He probably wondered if he would be called to account by the Egyptians for the murder of the Egyptian slave master. Moses learned that credibility and authority do not come from external things like speech. Instead, they come from deep convictions and consistency. Moses had both of these.

Sometimes, a chaplain is blessed with natural abilities in speaking or an impressive attractive appearance. These help to make a good initial impression and provide momentum for ministry. It is important to those so blessed that they not rely solely on their natural abilities but seek to build on them. A young chaplain came to a National Guard unit. He was handsome, athletic, and had a clear and resonant voice. He could think quickly and "on his feet." He made an enormous impression on people. Soon, the troops began to learn that he did not protect things told to him in confidence and did not follow up on promises he made. Colleagues learned that he would be late to meetings or miss them altogether. He could not be depended upon to complete assigned tasks. Superiors noticed that he did not think the standard rules applied to him. He was counseled and instructed. Finally, supervisors transferred him to a remote unit where teamwork was not as critical. This was an opportunity for him to get a new start with new insights and attitudes. He later resigned.

Personal characteristics as above have much to do with suitability for chaplain ministry. Academic and intellectual qualifications have much to do with a chaplain's ability to perform needed functions. College and seminary degrees are essential for theological preparation. Chaplains can make good use of skills of other disciplines such as psychology, sociology, philosophy, and history.

I learned that describing a patient's spiritual pilgrimage to the treatment team with terms from psychology or sociology often led to a more complete understanding by the health care professionals than if I had used theological language.

Students looking forward to a career in chaplaincy should take elective courses in other "helping professions." Clinical pastoral education (CPE) may be the most important ingredient of chaplain training. Valuable facets of CPE include the following. Analyzing and integrating the various disciplines mentioned above is a great benefit. An honest and courageous look at one's own beliefs and practices including contradictory concepts can be a life-changing process. Feedback from supervisors and other students is both challenging and affirming. Learning and practicing pastoral care skills can build confidence. For information about CPE, contact the Association for Clinical Pastoral Education.[13]

Every chaplain should take advantage of continuing education opportunities in order to strengthen skills and develop new ones. This should be a priority. Denominational conferences provide fresh ideas and also may be a time of reflection and retreat. Seminaries and other schools offer refresher courses.

Employers usually offer in-service training. These do not have to be about chaplain issues. One of the most helpful in-service courses I took dealt with medical terminology. Chaplains can gain much when learning about the principles and practices of other professionals such as psychologists, social workers, recreation leaders, and others.

Moses learned to live with his apparent disqualifications and to use the abilities he did have. Undertaking a task is difficult when one does not feel qualified. This is certainly a prime element in discerning and developing any type of ministry. Something can be said for going with your strengths, but this assumes we know our strengths and that we know what is needed for a task. Moses depended on God to show him not only what to do and say but also how to pursue God's calling. God knows of strengths and abilities that a chaplain can develop.

Moses' varied experiences combined to give him helpful insights. These insights would become helpful many years in the future, though he could not see it at the time.

When his parents told him of his rescue after his birth, he could not have seen the implications of this for his future. His education and training in the house of pharaoh's daughter gave him a grasp of Egyptian culture. This became valuable when he confronted pharaoh. Herding sheep must have been boring, challenging, uncomfortable, but instructive. These experiences worked to prepare him, though he probably had no cognizance of it.

Moses learned and continued to learn many things throughout his ministry. He learned from other people, including those who opposed him. He learned by reflecting on his experiences. He learned from failures and mistakes.

I tried several times to converse with a man in the long-term unit of a mental hospital. His slurred speech and soft voice made it difficult to understand his words. He was reluctant to talk at all. One day, he asked if we could talk. He seemed to be clear in thought and speech. I pulled a chair close and leaned toward him. Then I noticed an odor. The smell of urine attacked me so that I could hardly breathe. The overpowering odor nauseated me. I wanted to stay and listen, but I could not. Finally, I made an excuse, promised to return, and left. Subsequent efforts to talk with him failed. He no longer wanted to talk. I regret this failure.

During my intern year, I made mistakes in my contacts with patients. The supervisor and peer group helped me to see that. On a day in which I was painfully aware of making mistakes, the supervisor said, "You can learn more from mistakes than from successes, and since you are here to learn, that is a good thing."

CHAPTER 7

Moses Faced Opposition from Those in Power (Egyptians)

Pharaoh had all the power. Absolute power led to brutality. All male Israelite babies were ordered to be killed in order to limit the population growth. Workers and overseers were beaten when the work lagged. Long days without days off were the usual fare. Moses had no power, only influence. What Moses did have was the call and power of God. Pharaoh did not recognize God or God's power. Moses faced pharaoh to deliver God's demand that God's people be set free.

Slaves labored on massive building projects pharaoh was pursuing. The Israelite slaves were essential to pharaoh's plans. He had no reason to turn the people loose and every reason to hold on to them.

Moses took the elders with him when he first confronted pharaoh. God required pharaoh to let the people go. A warning was included in the message. Pharaoh belittled Moses and the message from God. Egypt had many gods. Why should pharaoh worry about this one? How crushing it must have been for Moses to see that his efforts were not only failing to succeed but also were making things worse. The people were given a quota of bricks to be made. Straw was needed and was provided. After the confrontation, pharaoh ordered the straw withheld, but the quota remained the same (Exodus 5:8–9, 7:25–8:15).

At long last, pharaoh finally agreed to the necessity of complying with God's demands to set the people free. Pharaoh was convinced only after the long struggle of plagues, which was difficult for both Egyptians and Israelites. At first, he ignored and ridiculed the plagues and Moses' claim that God wanted his people to be freed. When pharaoh began to see God's power demonstrated, he still refused. Later when he felt the pressure to comply, he became hostile and even more abusive.

After agreeing, pharaoh changed his mind several times when the pressure was relieved. Freedom came to the Israelites only after the Passover event. This convinced pharaoh that he could no longer resist. This powerful event deeply affected both Egyptians and Israelites. The event is celebrated to this day.

Sometimes, a chaplain's efforts to make improvements result in making things worse. Long range values are hard to see when short range difficulties mount. Chaplain ministries can sometimes take much longer than expected. We cannot assume that all the supervisors and elected or appointed officials are supportive. Some are openly opposed. One army chaplain was told by his commander, "Just stay out of my way." A hospice social worker was known to routinely tell patients the chaplain couldn't help them. The coworker who informed me of this would not tell me who the person was. I would have liked to have engaged the person in conversation to solve the problem and gain the cooperation of this person, but I could not. Sometimes, our detractors remain anonymous, so chaplains may need to build good relationships with all colleagues.

Chaplain Carl Hart, former director of chaplain services for the Home Mission Board of the Southern Baptist Convention, described this facet of prison ministry.

> The chaplain stands between the inmate and the outside world. He follows that narrow line between inmate and Warden, supporting both. He is not so conned by the inmate that he loses respect for the Warden, and he doesn't become a yes-man with the warden to the extent that the inmate has no confidence in him. He represents concern and interest in the individual in such a way that the inmate will see that somebody cares, and in so doing the chaplain shows the care and concern that God has for every individual.[14]

This in-between position applies to other forms of chaplaincy to a greater or lesser degree. Moses always seemed to be standing between God and pharaoh, God and the Israelites, or God and the Israelite leadership.

Chaplains often find themselves facing the in-between position. Military chaplains stand between officers and enlisted. Health care chaplains stand between physicians and patients. Hospice chaplains stand between patients and their families. Correctional chaplains stand between security staff and treatment staff or between staff and inmates. The awkwardness demands that the chaplain display patience, diplomacy, and consistency. Taking sides in "turf wars" will result in compromising the chaplain's role.

CHAPTER 8

Moses Worked with Peers Who Did Not Share His Vision (Israelite Leaders)

God gave Moses a vision. The vision was to set the people free. Even with God's help, Moses could not have accomplished the mission alone. He worked with the organization and structure that was already in place in the Israelite community.

Twelve tribes were formed from the descendants of Jacob's (Israel's) sons. There was loyalty within each tribe and sometimes conflict between tribes. The appointed elders were powerful and influential (Numbers 11). *Elder* is derived from a root word meaning "chin" or "beard." An elder then would be a grown man with a full beard. Rick Davies described elders as powerful in personality, prowess, and stature. They were influential members of powerful families. Elders demonstrated a wide range of authority numerous times throughout the Old Testament period. Rick Davies described them as lawmakers, men of valor, and connected to kings.[15] Pederson describes elders as those who upheld the community. Theirs was an image of elderly and wise men. Elders were a constant feature from the time of Moses to the time of Ezra.[16]

Priests were also active in the Israelite community. Raymond Abba described the role of Israelite priests at the time of Moses. Priests served a representation function. They represented the people. The essential function was to assure, maintain, and constantly reestablish the holiness of the elect people of God (Exodus 28:39, Leviticus 10:17). Priests maintained the sacrificial system, engaged in teaching and in revelation. They gave direction and guidance in the ordinary affairs of life.[17]

Israelite supervisors assigned by the Egyptians were placed over the Israelite workers. Supervisors were held accountable to ensure that the work was done.

> The Israelite foremen appointed by Pharaoh's slave drivers were beaten and were asked, "Why didn't you meet your quota of bricks yesterday or today, as before?" (Exodus 5:14)

The firmly established elders, priests, and supervisors exerted strong influence over the people. The exceedingly hard life was relatively stable and predictable. The people were acutely aware that their plight was getting worse with Moses' interventions. Elders and priests would have been fully aware of the worsening situation. They may have reflected the people's grave misgivings about Moses' actions. Moses knew that the elders and priests could make or break his efforts to do God's will. Moses was eventually able to convince them that God would work things out. The support of the leaders came and went with current events.

Moses learned to pursue the vision in spite of criticism. Decisions were based on God's guidance instead of the wishes of the people. Right decisions were more important than comfort and safety. Convinced that he was following God's will, Moses was able to move with confidence.

Differences of opinion can be complicated. My Army Reserve unit was a prisoner of war camp. We were deployed to Saudi Arabia during Operation Desert Shield/Desert Storm. United States forces and Saudi Arabian troops and civilian leaders were allies. The POW camp housed over ten thousand prisoners on Saudi soil. Differences in language, authority, leadership, culture, and religious practices complicated working relationships. Chaplains served a dual role. We ministered to the 1,500 US troops. We also offered ministry to the Iraqi prisoners.

A captain in the Saudi Army came to my tent after dark and asked to speak to me privately. He wanted our conversation to be confidential. He never told me his name. We talked about the Christian faith and the Bible. Both of us were courteous and respectful. I gave him a Bible and other literature.

The camp was located about halfway between the front lines and the rear area. Travelers found it convenient to stop for a meal and a night's rest. I think the visitor was one of the travelers. He visited four more times, always after dark. We explored questions regarding Christian beliefs in a way that was both cordial and which led to appreciation. Then he stopped coming. I don't know why. This example shows how differences, even wide differences, can be explored in a positive way. It does not always work out this way.

A physician in a hospital where I worked disagreed with the assistant superintendent (his supervisor) and mounted a semisecret campaign to get him fired. He asked me to support his position. I did not agree with his complaints and wrote a letter to him telling him my reasons. The situation became polarized, and we had several sharp conflicts. He would not speak to me and had negative things to say about me. I must admit I did not want to speak to him either. Later, this physician's son died. I wanted to offer my support but felt it would be rejected and make matters worse. I sent him a sympathy card assuring him of my prayers.

Chaplains may find that he or she is not getting the cooperation needed. Peers often give chaplaincy a lower priority than other programs. This attitude expresses itself in a variety of ways such as withholding needed supplies, delays in arranging activities, and outright refusal to cooperate. Psychiatric technicians assigned to accompany patients to the worship services had the responsibility to monitor patients' behavior. Most of the technicians helped with the services. Some said they enjoyed worshipping with the group. Others left the patients in the chapel to go outside and smoke cigarettes. This sometimes resulted in disruption in the service because of the lack of supervision. Challenging or criticizing the technicians would likely result in resentment. Instead, I routinely thanked them for their cooperation, even when less than it should be. Chaplains should give compliments to the supportive colleagues while trying to encourage the others. In time, this can have a positive effect.

Though some coworkers were not helpful, many others were. I was fortunate that in all the ministry settings I worked in, I found coworkers who supported the chaplain's ministry. A guard frequently came in on his own time and in civilian clothes to participate in chapel activities. I was fortunate that most of the hospice staff recognized the vital correlation of theological issues and end-of-life issues. So many referrals came to me that I often worked ten or twelve hours a day.

Chaplains who seek to please everyone soon become frustrated. Overemphasis on pleasing the people served leads a chaplain without clear direction. Overemphasis on pleasing superiors leads a chaplain unfulfilled. A delicate balance is needed. Moses continually sought to please God more than the people.

CHAPTER 9

Moses Served People Who Did Not Trust Him (Israelite People)

T he people longed for a place they had never known. They yearned to escape the anguish of slavery. Downtrodden, abused, and miserable, they dreamed of freedom and a "land of milk and honey."

> The Lord said, I have indeed seen the misery of my people in Egypt… So I have come down to rescue them from the hand of the Egyptians and to bring them up out of that land into a good and spacious land, a land flowing with milk and honey. (Exodus 3:7–8)

These words from Moses thrilled them, but many questions plagued them. Can this really be true? How can we know if Moses can do this? Can we believe what Moses says? Was it really God who sent Moses?

The people wavered back and forth from enthusiastic support of Moses to outright rebellion. At first, they were glad when Moses announced that God was going to set them free.

> Moses and Aaron brought together all the Elders of the Israelites and Aaron told them everything the Lord had said to Moses. He also performed the signs before the people, and they believed. And when they heard that the Lord was concerned about them and had seen their misery, they bowed down and worshipped. (Exodus 4:29–31)

When freedom did not come quickly, they began to criticize Moses. Things got worse for them. When pharaoh cancelled the provision of straw, forcing the Israelites to gather straw themselves, anger flared. The results of Moses' confrontation with pharaoh made their situation unbearable.

> The Israelite foremen realized they were in trouble when they were told "you are not to reduce the number of bricks required of you for each day". When... they found Moses and Aaron waiting to

meet them...they said, "You have made us a stench to Pharaoh and his officials and have put a sword in their hand to kill us." (Exodus 5:19–21)

Pharaoh's stubborn refusals prolonged the time needed to convince him to release them. The Israelites became impatient. Frustration resulted when they faced the menace of frogs, gnats, and other plagues. Blame and criticism increased toward Moses every time a problem emerged. After starting out on the journey, they considered relenting to serve the Egyptians.

As Pharaoh approached, the Israelites looked up, and there were the Egyptians marching after them. They were terrified and cried out to the Lord. They said to Moses, "Was it because there were no graves in Egypt that you brought us to the desert to die? What have you done to us by bringing us out of Egypt? Didn't we say to you in Egypt, leave us alone; let us serve the Egyptians? It would have been better to serve the Egyptians than to die in the desert. (Exodus 14:10–12)

Enthusiasm soared again after the Red Sea experience.

When the Israelites saw the great power of the Lord displayed against the

Egyptians, the people feared the Lord and put their trust in Him and in Moses His servant. (Exodus 16:31)

Unfortunately, this trust did not last long.

> They camped at Rephidim but there was no water for the people to drink. So they quarreled with Moses... Why did you bring us up out of Egypt to make us and our children and livestock die of thirst. (Exodus 17:1–3)

Moses faced this scenario multiple times while the group migrated in the desert. Trust in Moses needed to be there in order for the effort to succeed. A leader can do little unless he or she has committed followers.

Communication with the people was vital and difficult for several reasons. Minimal education of the people likely led to incomplete understanding. Large numbers of people required the relaying of Moses' words. The speech impediment may have led to misunderstanding. Location contributed to the complexity of Moses' leadership. Goshen was the area where the Israelite people lived. The valley was thirty to forty miles across. Getting an accurate message to the twelve tribes became uncertain.

Trust in another person stems from several factors. Knowing someone is helpful, but knowing a person is more than knowing about the person. Surely, the word about Moses' arrival and his quest to secure their freedom was widely known and talked about. Only a small percentage of them actually knew him. Direct communication contributes to an increased level of trust. Shared hopes and purposes bring valuable credibility which enhances trust. Experience with another can lead to confidence in that person. Confidence leads to trust. Trust affects all areas of chaplain ministry. Extreme diligence must be exercised to build and maintain trust.

Inmates and others often make false assumptions about chaplains. Many assume that he or she will report to officials what is told. Chaplains must maintain confidentiality in all but a few situations. Information affecting the safety of the institution should be shared. Some inmates have tried, before sharing, to extract a promise from me that I will not divulge information shared. I will never make that promise. Instead, I explain that I rarely share anything, but if something is said that must be told, I tell them, "I will go with you to share it with the security staff." Privileged communication becomes an issue at times. Various interpretations of the meaning and practice of the concept emerge. Catholic priests are forbidden to divulge under any circumstances what is told in a confessional. US Army Regulations (AR165-1) clearly outline the parameters of confidentiality for military chaplains.[18] Other faith groups do not appear to have a clear consensus. Laws vary from state to state. Chaplains must carefully research the laws, practices, policies, and ecclesiastical requirements. A clear and extensive written statement of a chaplain's policy regarding confidentiality done well in advance can avoid difficulties later.

Most organizations have an active "grapevine." Messages travel the grapevine with amazing rapidity. Rumors seem to appear out of nowhere. Much of what is heard is false or incomplete. Some are outright malicious. Chaplains must never pass along rumors. Even knowing that certain items are true does not justify the telling of it. Chaplains may have an opportunity to correct false and hurtful things that are told.

Chaplains may seek to build trust in the following ways. Confidentiality must be guarded. Respect should be displayed. Favoritism must be avoided. Ethics and values should be visible.

A critical need for trust in the chaplain emerges when an inmate approaches release. Inmates sincerely want to get out and stay out of prison. However, the transition is usually more difficult than they expect. A prison psychologist once said that the transition *out* of incarceration is nearly always harder than the transition *into* prison. Reasons for this are easy to see. Parole boards demand that released offenders not associate with former friends who have a record with law enforcement. Dysfunctional families do not help. Unresolved issues with families may complicate the return. Employers may be skeptical of former inmates. Few churches welcome recently released former inmates. Where does this leave the person? They may experience anxiety, loneliness, and depression. This may lead them to conclude that they cannot make it in the free world.

Chaplains may be able to help with this difficult process. I often tried to connect an inmate with a church in the community where he was to be released. Hopefully, he would make friends at church who would be a good influence. The sensitivity of this process requires extreme care. Only the pastor and a few parishioners should be aware of the person's background. The former inmate should be the one who decides when and what to share. I recommended that they get comfortable with new friends before sharing their history. Limited success was achieved in this effort. Much stress and anxiety was felt by the former inmate. Confidentiality became hard to preserve. Friendly people in the church innocently inquired about his background. Sometimes, the church connection was short term. Even with the uncertainties, there were some who successfully integrated back into the "free world." Every success was a blessing.

CHAPTER 10

Moses Experienced Changes

The popular statement "one thing that never changes is the inevitability of change" rings true for most organizations. Chaplains have no choice but to face changes. The variety of changes makes it impossible to predict.

Egypt was a different place when Moses returned. Many changes occurred in forty years. The new pharaoh in power did not seem to know anything about Moses' history. Pharaoh could have used Moses' murder of the Egyptian against him if he had known. Moses could have been executed, thus ending the challenge to pharaoh. There is no mention of Moses' stepmother, pharaoh's daughter. Brutality and mistreatment almost certainly escalated during forty years. His mother, Jochobed, and his father, Amram, were probably no longer alive since their names were not mentioned after Moses' return to Egypt. Israelite leaders showed no indication that they remembered Moses.

Throughout the exodus and throughout his life, Moses experienced many changes. Some were sudden and unexpected while others were gradual and predictable. Some were dreaded while others were intentionally sought after. Some were in response to events or needs. Some were eagerly hoped for. Freedom for the Israelites was a huge change. Four or five generations produced a people who had never seen the Promised Land—only heard about it.

My oldest daughter was seven years old when we moved from Georgia to Kansas City to attend seminary. As a family, we often talked about returning home to Georgia. After five years, she had lived in Missouri almost as long as she had lived in Georgia and remembered very little of Georgia. The other children remembered almost nothing of Georgia. When our children would lead in prayer, they often said something about "going home to Georgia."

Moving to the Promised Land was a long cherished dream for the people. They yearned for it, but a massive change would be needed. Moses spent nearly forty years preparing the people for this change. Resistance to change was also part of the picture. Consciously or unconsciously, many of the people feared leaving the familiar for the uncertain. Their initial enthusiasm changed as they suffered through the plagues. A degree of comfort comes from knowing what to expect even in a miserable situation.

During the time I served as a prison chaplain, the mission and philosophy went through radical changes every two to four years. Each change brought different policies, procedures, personnel, and inmates. Changes to chapel activities were necessary and not welcome. Adapting to the new environment required patience and innovation. I was grateful to see God's ministry flourish in each new environment.

Chaplains will face things that need to be changed such as discriminatory policies, manipulations of clients and staff, and even abuse. Chaplains can be change agents by working within the system to influence those who can make decisions for change. This requires balance between aggressive action and ongoing gradual change. Influence provides more progress than power plays. Gradually influencing one coworker at a time can build a positive foundation for permanent change. Chaplains are appropriate agents for change. Virtually, every major rehabilitation program in corrections was started by faith groups. "Penitentiary" began as "a place to be penitent."

Changes can also occur in people. Many corrections employees do not believe that inmates will change. This attitude expresses itself in disrespect and harshness toward inmates. In turn, this treatment makes it harder for an inmate who really does want to change. Some inmates do change.

A twenty-year-old newly assigned inmate came to me and said he had become a Christian and would like to be baptized. This was not unusual. Some inmates did this hoping that I would write a letter to the parole board. I always told them my policy was never to write the parole board. For those who continued in their request, I had a plan. I gave them reading material, posing questions that

I felt certain they could not answer. I hoped they would struggle with the answers. After weeks and subsequent sessions, I could be confident of their sincerity. This young man persisted and told me how he made the commitment. He was in a county jail after sentencing and before going to the reception center. He told me a man came to the jail regularly and preached to the inmates. There was no chapel, but he preached in a hallway where the cells fronted and the inmates could hear through the bars. Some inmates yelled insults and profanities; others ignored him. This young man ignored him at first but then began to listen. Privately, he made the commitment and later shared with the preacher. I decided to set up the baptism. I located the man doing the preaching. He said he had been doing that for years but did not recall this young man. The preacher attended the baptism which was a joyous celebration. The preacher was encouraged as he recalled the words of the Apostle Paul.

> I planted the seed, Apollos watered it, but God made it grow. (1 Corinthians 3:6)

Chaplains should believe that people can change. This is the premise of the Christian gospel. Chaplains should give encouragement to clients as they strive to change.

My youngest son convinced me that change is not only possible but also likely when others believe in them. When his wife called us to reveal that our son was using drugs, we were devastated. My first move was to call a friend who served as chaplain in a drug rehabilitation center. That chaplain put me in touch with an experienced therapist. The therapist coached us through an intervention process. Our son then enrolled in an outpatient program. His wife told him, "If you relapse, it will be over for us." Five months later, he did relapse. Wife, house, job, and even his dog were all gone. He hit bottom. Then on suicide watch in an inpatient program, he began to get serious about changing. As I write this, twenty-seven years later, he remains drug free. He is also highly committed to helping others to stay clean. One mother told my wife that our son had saved her son's life when he helped him give up drugs. Positive change can be more than mere survival. It can be a source of fulfillment.

Reinhold Neibuhr, a Presbyterian minister, wrote a prayer in 1947 that may be instructive to chaplains. The prayer has been used by many twelve-step groups.

God, grant me the serenity to accept the things I cannot change, the courage to change the things I can, and the wisdom to know the difference.

CHAPTER 11

Moses Struggled with Uncertainty

We want our world to be clear. Decisions need adequate information. Responsibilities need knowledge of parameters. Problems need understanding of expectations. Accomplishment needs vision. Values like these are hard to come by. We live with uncertainties, some of which are troubling. Moses struggled with uncertainties. A few of them are as follows.

Several commentators support the view that Moses' stepmother planned to groom him to be pharaoh (Charles Swindoll, Josephus). Opposition would have emerged from factions among the Egyptians. His future in Egypt was uncertain. The Red Sea loomed as a formidable barrier. How could Moses be certain that God would intervene? What would happen? Midian was a new place to him. How could he develop confidence that Jethro and Midianite society would accept him? Egypt was different when Moses returned. How could he know what to expect? Twelve spies returned with mixed messages after surveying the land of Canaan. How could Moses decide the best course of action?

Scriptures give the impression that Moses' decisions were clear. They were not. The biblical accounts were written many years later from the perspective of history. Moses' struggles with uncertainty abounded in numerous events such as how to respond to the idolatry with the golden calf and the Israelites' threats to turn back to serve pharaoh.

Moses faced uncertainty by keeping a strong belief that God would lead him to the right decisions. His call and his relationship with God bolstered Moses' confidence (Exodus 5:22, 6:10–12, 10:29).

Chaplains face uncertainty many times and in many ways. Governmental programs come and go quickly, especially those based on grants.

My family encountered uncertainty many times. The move to Kansas City, the move to north Georgia, the move to Florida, and the move to Alabama were stressful because of uncertainty. We made the decisions without the full information we wanted. Some decisions were made suddenly.

Uncertainty occurred when the end of the CPE residency approached and I sought permanent employment. Two new prisons were opening. One in north Georgia and one in South Georgia would be hiring chaplains. I applied for both positions. The interviewer said I could not apply to both. I must choose at that very moment. I had little information about the communities where these were located. How could I make a decision which would affect my family for years?

Uncertainties occurred during my deployment during Operation Desert Shield/Desert Storm. Two chaplains held Christian worship services for the prisoner of war camp in Saudi Arabia. Guards escorted prisoners to the location. We sought interpreters but found few. I asked the group, "Who speaks English?" Nobody volunteered, but they pointed to each other. I gathered behind me those who were pointed out so they could interpret. Each time I made a statement, they discussed it. A simple statement such as "God is good" resulted in several minutes of discussion, and then one of them repeated the statement in Arabic. All this produced uncertainty. Did they understand? What was really repeated to the congregation? We adapted elements of the worship service to enhance communication. We taught them two songs in English: "Alleluia" consisted of only one word and "God Is So Good" used only four. The songs, sung with gusto, added to the worship. We recited the Lord's Prayer; they in Arabic, and we in English. The difficulty was explaining what I wanted them to do. One worship service illustrates the uncertainty. On that day, the guards kept busy controlling a disturbance and could not escort the prisoners. My chaplain's assistant gathered eight of them and escorted them. None of them spoke English. They did not sing. They did not pray, nothing communicated. I abandoned any effort at a sermon. I walked to each individual, placed my hand on his head, and prayed aloud for him. I left, thinking it was a waste of time. Later, reflection convinced me I should not consider an effort worthless just because I did not understand.

Uncertainty sprang up when the news media reported that the mental hospital where I worked might be closed. Rumors spread far and wide. Nothing was clear. Employee morale plummeted. Anxiety skyrocketed. A long six months passed before the uncertainty cleared.

CHAPTER 12

Moses Faced Shortages of Resources

Estimates of the number of people leaving Egypt range widely from six hundred thousand to over a million. Exodus 12:37 indicates that six hundred thousand men were included, not counting women and children. Just feeding the people in the desert was a logistical nightmare. At first, the cattle and grain sufficed. When food began to run out, the need became urgent, and the people complained. When water was no longer available, the need became critical. The Israelites demanded that Moses do something. Moses asked God for help. Solutions came in ways no one could ever have imagined. Water from a rock? Bread from a substance found on the ground? Clearly, the provision was from God.

Budgets are almost always projected one or two years in advance. The budget approvals come only after a close look at needs and priorities. Generally, various departments overestimate needs resulting in budget makers having to reduce amounts. In some cases, chaplains' budgets receive lower priority. Vehicles, furniture, and other tangible items are more easily justified than expenses for a chaplain. When budgets are finalized, there may be additional cuts at the time for disbursements.

Chaplains want to urge that their budgets be given a high priority. Efforts to achieve this are easily misunderstood. Political maneuvers, complaints, manipulation, or any sort of pressure tactic usually result in temporary improvement. No method works perfectly, but here are some ideas that may help.

1. Keep supervisors informed of the values of chaplain ministry. Do this all year, not just at budget time. Monthly reports, informal conversations, photos, and worship programs can be helpful.
2. Try to understand and be sympathetic to the pressure on administrators to hold down expenses. Let them know you realize they have other employees wanting something from them and that you don't expect special treatment.
3. Include supervisors in chaplain activities so they can see the merits firsthand. I frequently invited my superiors to assist with serving communion or to attend an Easter service.

4. Be willing to compromise. Partial funding is a reason for gratitude.

5. Show genuine appreciation for efforts. When an administrator sees your gratitude, he may be more amenable later on.

6. Provide pastoral care for administrators when they face difficulties if possible. Each time I was moved to a new Army Reserve unit or whenever a new commander was assigned, I would request a private meeting. After assuring him of my support, I would say something like, "I want to be your chaplain too. I'll be glad to meet with you confidentially any time you feel the need. We can meet at a time and place that will be comfortable." Several of them took me up on the offer.

Sometimes, resources can come from sources a chaplain would not expect. We did not have enough hymnals, and the ones we had were not the kind we needed. Money was not available to purchase them. A call came from a denominational official inviting me to participate in a "Christmas in August" emphasis. This nationwide program recruited young ladies in churches to encourage their church members to purchase items to be donated. I told them the name and edition of the hymnal. Generous donations provided enough hymnals with some to spare.

A hospital I served urgently needed a chaplain for the children and youth units. Years of requests, analysis, and justifications failed to get another chaplain. One day, a member of the pastoral services advisory board asked me,

"What is your greatest need?" Without any realistic expectation of success, I answered him. I told him we needed another chaplain and why. As it turned out, he was on the boards of several charitable foundations. He suggested I apply for a couple of grants and coached me through the application process. The grants were approved, and a chaplain was hired. Three years later, before the grants expired, the state created a permanent position.

Moses learned that solutions may come in unexpected ways. God told Moses to strike a rock, and when he did, water flowed and the crisis was averted (Exodus 17:5–6). Food was running out. Moses showed them that God was providing food. A substance was found on the ground they called manna. This manna could be gathered and made into bread. Quail appeared each evening. No one could have expected the manna or the quail (Exodus 16:11–14). Perhaps, the manna and quail had always been there. We don't know. Moses emphasized that it was God who provided. The people agreed but soon forgot. Chaplains must not limit thinking to ordinary solutions. We should be aware of opportunities and open to solutions we would not expect.

CHAPTER 13

Moses Coped with Overwhelming Demands

The next day Moses took his seat to serve as judge for the people, and they stood around him from Morning till evening.

—Exodus 18:13

Moses was wearing down from trying to meet the massive needs of his people. His close relationship with God equipped Moses to give wise counsel. However, the workload was too heavy. Moses counseled the people giving guidance regarding personal decisions, family issues, problem solving, disputes, and spiritual issues. It was more than Moses could handle. Jethro, Moses' father-in-law, recognized the problem, though Moses probably did not. Jethro predicted that both Moses and the people would wear out. Moses' father-in-law had a good solution. He said Moses should delegate duties to capable men at various levels of responsibility. These men were probably the elders.

> Teach them the decrees and laws, and show them the way to live and the duties they are to perform. Select capable men from all the people, men who fear God, trustworthy men who hate dishonest gain and appoint them as officials over thousands, hundreds, fifties and tens. Have them serve as judges for the people at all times, but have them bring every difficult case to you. If you do this and God so commands, you will be able to stand the strain, and all these people will go home satisfied. (Exodus 18:20–21)

Most chaplains have times of feeling overwhelmed when the workload seems impossible. This takes a toll on the chaplain as well as the effectiveness of the ministry. Not only do some needs go unmet, but also some things are done hurriedly or poorly. Counseling sessions are rushed, and sermons and Bible studies fail to get thoroughly prepared.

Chaplains can also face needs that he or she cannot meet. An eight-year-old boy had just died. He was the only child of his mother who was hysterical and screaming when I arrived. I used every skill I possessed, but she continued to yell and scream. A phrase she used bothered me. She continued to say, "Goddamn, God." I knew my job was not to evaluate her theology but to offer care and concern. It wasn't working. Soon, a priest arrived. He said almost nothing but immediately started praying aloud. He repeated the familiar prayers that all Catholics memorize. This continued for thirty or forty minutes. She eventually joined in the prayers and finally calmed down. I learned that she found help in the familiar rituals of her faith, not in my efforts.

All this contributes to "chaplain burnout." The gradual process can feed feelings of frustration. Chaplains should be alert for signs which might be subtle. Consider the gas gauge in your car. Looking at it will prevent running out of gas. The gauge will only work if it is looked at. Rarely will agencies provide adequate coverage to meet all needs. So chaplains will need to solve this for themselves. See chapter 16 for ways to prevent burnout.

Jethro's advice still works today as chaplains utilize volunteers. Volunteers can be a tremendous benefit in both quantity of services and quality of services. Volunteers can serve as individuals or can come as a group. Churches provided choirs and other types of groups. Four functions are essential for effective volunteer ministry. They are recruitment, training, organization, and supervision. Careful attention should be given to each of these functions.

1. Individual volunteers can be recruited from a variety of sources. Colleges and seminaries are valuable sources. I have been fortunate to work with interns in chaplaincy, criminal justice, and sociol-

ogy programs. Interns are usually well motivated, well educated, and have the advantage of being accountable to the sponsoring school. Churches are also good sources, but careful screening must be done. Certainly, a volunteer being considered for a maximum security prison will need more screening than one who will sing in a nursing home. Recruitment screening should evaluate whether the skills, insights, and personality mesh well with the tasks. Some volunteers may have skills in music or art. Others may be good listeners. Some may relate only to their own age range. Others function best in groups.

I conducted a devotional service each week in the long-term care program at the mental hospital. Whenever there were five Wednesdays in a month, I would invite a minister of music from a local church to lead a sing-along. A remarkable thing frequently happened at these sing-alongs.

Patients who were usually withdrawn and non-communicative would sing along and occasionally get up and sing a solo. The volunteers touched a healthy part of the patients through music.

Groups can also provide valuable service. Functions such as musical presentations, Bible study classes, participating in worship, and dramatic programs have many advantages. Careful attention should be paid to ensure that leaders are aware of all guidelines and communicate them to group members.

Volunteers can recruit other volunteers. These usually are effective volunteers and may not require as much orientation.

2. Training is essential. Poor training is unfair to the volunteer and counterproductive to the setting. Written guidelines should be provided and reviewed with prospects. I have heard a few chaplains say, "I don't have time to train volunteers. I could do the task myself in less time than it takes to train someone." This may be true early on, but when fully prepared, a volunteer can give as much as ten hours of service for each hour of training invested by a chaplain. Volunteer training is well worth the effort.

3. Organization, including communication, helps everyone understand the expectations, limits, procedures, and accountability. Conflicting or confusing information erodes the enthusiasm of volunteers.

4. Supervision must be consistent and understood by the volunteer. I made it a priority to meet and greet each volunteer if possible each time they visited. While thanking the volunteer for their service, I often gained feedback on how their service was going. Violations of guidelines must be dealt with clearly and kindly. During the 1970s, some women started going without a bra. One young lady came to a group meeting a couple of times without a bra. This is not appropriate for a men's prison. She was a good volunteer, and I did not

want to lose her. I was getting ready to talk to her when another female volunteer came to me and said she would talk to her. She continued to attend but dressed more appropriately. Because the intervention was done by another volunteer, embarrassment was avoided.

Volunteers also improve the quality of chaplaincy services. Inmates often do not share truthfully with the chaplain because they fear what might be written in the record. Deep personal feelings may be easier to share with a volunteer.

A special Volunteer Appreciation Day was held each year to express thanks to volunteers. Certificates were given to outstanding volunteers and groups. A "Volunteer of the Year" was chosen by a committee. These occasions were always times of celebration and fellowship.

CHAPTER 14

Moses Dealt with Delays

Forty years elapsed before the Israelites set foot in the promised land. The direct route distance was about two hundred miles, and the distance by way of Mount Sinai was about four hundred miles. The trip could have been made in just a few months. A workable plan was ready. Moses was ready. Why then was there such a long delay? The people were not ready.

They were not ready for several reasons. Part of the reason for the delay was because they took the longer route toward the Red Sea instead of the more direct route through Philistine territory. Had they taken the more direct route, they almost certainly would have had to do battle with the Philistines. They were not prepared for war and were afraid of the experienced soldiers of the Philistines. God did not want the Israelites to take on the Philistines because He did not want them to turn back (Exodus 13:17–18).

Trust in Moses and faith in God needed to mature. The needed trust included two applications. They needed to be convinced that the purpose of the venture was to fulfill the promise given to Abraham centuries earlier. That purpose was to make Israel a great nation and bless the nations of the world.

They also needed to trust that Moses would lead them in the right direction. The Israelites needed to believe that Moses was acting on instructions from God.

Respect for "the Law" needed to be more widely recognized. In Egypt, they had been ruled by the fickle desires of the Egyptian overlords. Now they needed to be ruled by the Law which was given by God in a powerful way (Exodus 19:16–21).

Worship needed to be structured and practiced. They found it hard to believe that God would help them succeed. They lacked the faith to move forward. They preferred instead to remain in the unchallenged nomadic desert existence rather than risk challenging the current residents of Canaan.

They listened to the wrong people. Ten of the twelve men who saw the land gave a negative report based on fear. The majority opinion is not always right.

Moses learned patience through this and other delays. We cannot be sure how much time passed with the plagues. Clearly, the living conditions got worse for the Israelites as time and the plagues wore on. Sometimes, change is more effective when proceeding slowly. New habits and new understandings must be internalized to result in permanent change. If pharaoh had released the Israelites quickly, it might have been too easy if they failed to see their release as the work of God.

Eager and enthusiastic young chaplains often feel dismay over the slow pace of institutional change. Even changes that are clearly needed and supported by a majority come to fruition slowly or not at all. Governmental budgets are projected two or three years in advance. Needed funding that make it into budgets may still be a long time coming.

Chaplains, like Moses, must exercise patience. Delays are not excuses for failing to perform needed ministry. Sometimes, chaplains may need to minister in less than ideal circumstances. At other times, a chaplain can improvise in order to accomplish tasks.

Hospital worship services were normally held in a third floor conference room. One Sunday, I arrived to learn that the only elevator was broken. Many patients were unable to climb the stairs. Other conference rooms were too small. Eventually, we settled on a wide hallway leading to the dining hall. We had the service without a piano, without hymnals, and with only half enough chairs. The patients did not mind, and the worship went well.

An unexpected benefit was that dietary employees walking through the hall stopped and observed the worship. One commented that she had never attended a patient worship service before and appreciated the opportunity.

CHAPTER 15

Moses Accepted Disappointment

A great many disappointments came to Moses. Some of them were exceedingly bitter and long-lasting while others were temporary.

Chaplains need to realize that they personally are not the only ones facing difficulty. Chaplains may come to feel what I call the "isolation syndrome." Four ways of thinking contribute to this problem: first, the idea that others do not understand; second, the idea that no one else can do what you do; third, the idea that you should know everything and do everything; fourth, the idea others cannot help you. To those who experience this syndrome, I say, "You are not alone." There are those who understand and who can walk with you through this journey. A man I will call Walter (not his real name) was a person who walked with me. I was assigned to a new prison being built as my first assignment after completing a chaplain internship. The state prison system was assuming control of a small and old county work camp. A new building was almost complete, so the thirty county prisoners with short-term and misdemeanor sentences were left to help furnish and prepare the new building for occupancy.

On short notice, the state assumed control on a Friday afternoon. There was a small chapel on the property in a separate building, so I decided to hold a worship service on Sunday. I needed to have a pianist. Since I was in process of moving to the area, I knew no one. I called a local church, and the pastor referred me to a young man. This young man brought his father, Walter, when he came to play. Walter and I became friends. The new prison experienced much confusion with temporary workers from other prisons competing to have their ideas implemented. I was frustrated. Walter and I talked many times. Counseling was not his gift, but he listened, and he cared. We remained friends until he died fifteen years later.

Moses was not defeated by disappointments but learned important lessons. He put them into a forward-looking perspective. When things went wrong, he learned to adapt strategies. He shared his frustrations with God and with some of his coworkers. Though some things were unsuccessful, Moses found comfort in successes.

Perhaps, Moses expected that the process of convincing pharaoh would be quick and smooth. That was not to be. Instead, pharaoh's angry threats escalated with each new plague. Disappointment compounded for Moses, but he remained focused to his God-given quest. When pharaoh finally yielded, Moses likely felt vindication. Confidence in the plan increased for Moses and the Israelites after each setback was overcome.

Surely, the negative report from the spies and the people's refusal to move forward was a deep disappointment (Deuteronomy 1). His life's work and God's call now came to a halt. To his credit, Moses continued to lead the people. He could have split the group by taking those willing to go forward and leaving the others in the desert. Moses chose unity for the people over his own convictions. The needs of the people came before his own desires.

The bitterest disappointment of all had to be coming down the mountain after receiving the Ten Commandments to find the people worshipping the golden calf (Exodus 32). That period of time was the greatest event in his life and the worst. What an immense privilege to be in the very presence of God and to receive the Ten Commandments. Can you imagine the shock and anger Moses felt upon seeing his own brother, his closest ally, leading the people worshipping an idol Aaron had made? Abandoning God for idolatry was so evil that it called for a severe response. God was ready to destroy the people, but Moses interceded for them. Instead, Moses ordered two punishments. First, Moses ground the golden calf into powder, mixed it with the water, and made them drink it. Second, Moses instructed the Levites to go through the camp and kill certain people. Presumably, those three thousand were those who led the people astray. As severe as this slaughter was, it may be similar to a surgeon cutting out a cancerous tumor so that the rest of the body can be healthy.

Modern-day people may find it incredible to see what the people did when they worshiped the golden calf. We wonder why they resorted to this after witnessing God's miracles. Sacrificing of calves was a popular practice of the Egyptians. Israelites surely observed this practice and perhaps engaged in it themselves. Tremendous stress was on them as they waited at length for Moses to return from the mountain. They looked for comfort in something familiar even if it was destructive.

Those who work in addiction recovery programs are painfully aware of the powerful tendency to relapse under pressure. Chaplains must recognize this dynamic and not give up on someone who relapses. Many participants in twelve-step programs relapse several times before gaining control over their addiction. Moses was disappointed and angry, but he did not give up on the people or Aaron.

Disappointment never defeated Moses. Most of Moses' disappointments eventually resulted in change for the better. This was not easy or accidental. Changes came because Moses was able to see beyond the immediate crisis.

Disappointments will come to every chaplain. Some will be deeply painful, but they do not have to defeat us. We can be disappointed at a variety of circumstances, many of which are beyond our control. Here are some disappointments I have experienced or heard about.

My older son worked in a group home for troubled teenaged boys. One day, he called me and said, "Two big things happened today. First, when grade reports came out, all the boys showed improvement, some remarkably so. Second, the state announced that the group home would be closed. The center was being closed in order to save money. This was disappointing not only to my son but also to other staff and supervisors who had invested much time and energy in guiding these boys. The boys may have been discouraged because just when things were looking better, they would now have to adjust to something else."

An inmate who was a practicing Christian corresponded with a church. He asked them to pray for him. The church wrote him and said they had prayed and were convinced he would be released before his sentence expired. Early releases were used occasionally to reduce prison population. This inmate did not meet the criteria. The hope was unrealistic, but the inmate bought into it with enthusiasm. He believed if he had enough faith, he would be released. When it did not happen, he became severely discouraged. It was a theological crisis for him. I had several lengthy counseling sessions with him before he came to a more realistic perspective.

Events in a chaplain's area are often a mixture of positive and negative. I have rarely heard from former inmates. One young man contacted me occasionally. He was a new Christian and had a lot of interest in discipling new Christians. Books and articles I gave him were studied. A few years after his release, he started a group home for recovering addicts. What a joy when he called and said a local church planned to ordain him to the ministry and invited me to participate. It was thrilling to experience the "laying on of hands" (see Acts 6:5–6).

A bright young lady is released from the mental hospital only to commit suicide by setting herself on fire. A trusted coworker is arrested for child abuse. A volunteer goes on a campaign to get a chaplain fired. An inmate who appeared to be a committed Christian is released and immediately commits a violent crime. A governor of a state eliminates all chaplain positions and replaces them with untrained contract chaplains.

In difficult cases like these, a chaplain may be tempted to think, *If only I*. or, *I should have*. Hindsight is almost always clearer than foresight, but that is no reason for a chaplain to get into self-blaming.

A few years from retirement, my wife and I bought property and had plans drawn for a retirement home. Then the state decided to downsize the hospital where I worked. Smaller departments were combined into one, and the directors' positions were abolished. My position as director of pastoral services was abolished. At the age of fifty-nine and a half, I was unemployed. I was too young to retire and too old for a career change. Months went by, and applications for positions that I felt well qualified for were ignored. I became discouraged and wondered, *Have I outlived my usefulness?* My wife and I went on a retreat to the Smoky Mountains where we camped, talked, prayed, and considered our options. We made lists of places and positions where we did and did not want to go. Then a remarkable thing happened. I am convinced that God was behind it. A résumé was accidently misdirected from the hospice where I had sent it to another hospice. The second hospice, which was in Florida, offered me a job. We sold our home and the retirement property and moved again. Florida was on our list of places we did not want to go. We learned (again) not to get too tied up in our own wishes.

I learned that in hospice ministry, gray hair and age are not disqualifications. The hospice ministry was a wonderful way to complete my career. I felt appreciation and affirmation from patients, families, and staff. The ministry became the most rewarding of any in my career.

Hopefully, your ministry will balance feelings of satisfaction with the inevitable disappointments. Disappointments can lead to discouragement, which is the belief that things will not get better. Discouragement can lead to negative interpretations which may be difficult to move beyond. Feelings of failure can lower a chaplain's expectations; feelings of unworthiness can lower a chaplain's self-esteem. Feelings of isolation can lead to stress. Stress can lead to depression. Depression can lead to thoughts of giving up. Depression can take a heavy toll on chaplains and their families. It also has a negative effect on the ministry.

Most endorsing agencies offer chaplains free and confidential counseling. Employee assistance programs are also available from most employers. Disappointment, when not loaded with discouragement, can lead to positive responses. Reflect on a football team. They worked hard all year, maintained discipline, revised game plans, trusted their coach, and won many games. Now they play for the championship. They lose! How should they respond? They can evaluate. They can plan for next year. They can learn lessons. Most helpfully, they can celebrate the success. Chaplains may feel discouraged at times. Hopefully, they can respond like the ball team to recognize and celebrate successes. Then they can turn discouragement into encouragement which is the belief that things can get better.

Chaplains facing disappointments and discouragements like these have no guarantee that things will eventually work out. Disappointments may lead to discouragement, but they need not defeat us.

Focusing on the ministry rather than failures is a primary way to maintain motivation. This is stressful and confusing, so chaplains should give high priority to taking care of themselves.

CHAPTER 16

Moses Learned to Take Care of Himself

Throngs of people came to Moses with a myriad of demands. Conflicts, complaints, questions, and much more were the daily fare for him. This exhausting process must have taken a toll on Moses. The physical and emotional drain could have devastated him. Moses learned some ways to take care of himself.

A network of supportive, caring people helped to ease the burdens Moses carried. Older brother Aaron and older sister Miriam seem to be part of the day-in, day-out activities. They were an integral part of Moses' ministry. Music, dancing, and celebration were a healthy part of their relationship (Exodus 15:19–20). These enjoyable times may well have worked to relieve stresses that Moses encountered.

Jethro, Moses' father-in-law, gave much advice and encouragement. Since there is no mention of Moses' relationship with his father, he likely saw Jethro as a father figure. In addition to the visit previously mentioned, Jethro visited Moses several times and blessed him.

Moses occasionally took time to go away into a mountain by himself. Several times, God directed Moses to do so before important events. After years of the solitary life of a shepherd, Moses may have yearned for time to himself. Time alone with God gave Moses perspective. Time with others gave him support. Managing one's own emotions can be much like a bank account. Bank accounts are handy tools for managing money. However, they only work when things are kept in balance. Fees and frustration result when numbers do not balance. If more is going out of the account than is coming in, problems will surface. Consistent awareness and regular actions are necessary. Before writing a check, one should make sure funds are available. Periodic balancing will provide accurate information.

Emotional bank accounts fit the above pattern except that they are less obvious. When emotional energy is spent, it must be replaced. Otherwise, a deficit will emerge, and the chaplain may not have the emotional energy to respond helpfully when an urgent need arises. Some pastoral encounters are joyous and generate emotional energy. Deaths, funerals, death messages, suicide threats, and other negative encounters use up considerable amounts of time and energy.

A chaplain once told me that whenever he had a stressful pastoral care event, he would—if possible—spend an equal amount of time by himself, reflecting, meditating, or journaling. Unfortunately, this may not always be possible. We should try to reflect soon in order to reenergize. Retreats and conferences are effective ways to reflect.

Physical exercise can be an important way to relieve stress and evaluate priorities. Driving home from the prison where I worked, I passed through a large park with hiking trails and sidewalks. I usually stopped, changed clothes in the old Volkswagen van, and then jogged 2.3 miles before continuing home. Upon arriving home, I would be less stressed and more energetic both physically and emotionally. Then I would usually get into one of the many household projects I wanted to do. On those days when I did not stop and jog, I would generally become a couch potato.

Support groups are probably the most effective method of caring for oneself. Trust, encouragement, and feedback provided in a group are unsurpassed. Support groups have many different styles, formats, and personalities. Some are sponsored or recommended by denominations. Others may be an informal group of local ministers. Many books are available for guidance. If a chaplain cannot find a group, then he or she should start one. A pattern for a support group can be found in CPE groups.

Managing the time is an important discipline for avoiding fatigue and burnout. Chaplains are a convenient place for local churches and other groups to look for supply preaching. Some chaplains take on interim pastor positions. Churches and other organizations often recruit chaplains to serve on boards and committees or to provide training for church leaders. Before agreeing to take on additional responsibilities, a chaplain should assess the amount of time and emotional energy required. Ask yourself, "Does this activity lie at the heart of my ministry?" Spiritual vitality cannot be taken for granted. Regular and consistent use of spiritual resources can enhance a sense of spiritual well-being. Spiritual resources may include personal prayer, reflection, fellowship, worship, Bible reading, and relationships with trusted friends.

I wanted to have some private time of prayer before beginning my workday. The entrance to the chapel and my office connected to a multipurpose room. Inmates were allowed in this room at certain times. When I arrived each morning, there would usually be several inmates waiting at the door preventing me from having my quiet time. I decided to arrive thirty minutes sooner before the inmates had access to the chapel. My day got off to a better start after this.

Participation in a congregation apart from the chaplain setting can nurture faith and fellowship. A chaplain needs opportunities for fellowship, worship, and spiritual discipline in a setting he or she is not responsible for. I believe that a chaplain's spiritual ministry will not progress beyond the level of his or her own spiritual life.

CHAPTER 17

Moses Believed in a Future He Would Not See

Go up to the top of Pisgah and look west and north and south and east. Look at the land with your own eyes, since you are not going to cross this Jordan. But commission Joshua, and encourage and strengthen him, for he will lead this people across and will cause them to inherit the land that you will see.

—Deuteronomy 3:27–28

Moses kept his focus on the ultimate goal prescribed by God. The long-term goal of bringing the Israelites to the promised land determined the short-term goals. The tabernacle, the law, the organization, the leadership, and other directions set patterns to be used when the Israelites settled in Canaan. Moses learned much through this process.

Moses learned that God's work is not dependent on any single individual however worthy, faithful, or skilled that person might be. The chaplain who makes everything depend on him is setting up his or her successor to fail.

Seeing the promised land from a distance while knowing he would never enter it was a huge disappointment, and he possibly felt resentment. Hopefully, Moses took comfort in the knowledge that the mission would succeed without him.

Moses knew that a different set of skills would be needed by the leaders when taking over the land of Canaan. Capable warriors would be needed in order to succeed. When an administrative unit in the US Army is converted to an infantry unit, changes in chaplain assignments may be needed. A younger chaplain may relate better to the younger, more physically fit soldiers. Moses learned that a time would come to turn the task over to someone else. That someone was Joshua, and Moses knew it. He could have resented losing his leadership role. Instead, Moses prepared Joshua and blessed him in the presence of the people. Moses also prepared the people and blessed the people.

A seventy-eight-year-old man in a church I served as pastor told me he spent the day planting pine trees on unused farm land. Twenty years later, the trees could be harvested. He had to know he would not be the person to harvest them. This man saw the importance of leaving something for the future.

Leaving a place of service after a significant period of time can be difficult. Chaplains can respond to this issue in several helpful ways. Awareness in advance that at some date your service will be over may ease the grief when it occurs. Preparing and giving your blessing may help you affirm your legacy. Making the ministry depend heavily on the chaplain is a mistake. A heavy workload for you and struggles for your successor are results.

Records, policies, history, and other information should be made available to your successor but without any expectation that they will be adopted. The best tribute to your career is not how much you are missed but how little.

CHAPTER 18

Moses and Jesus

A comparison of the life of Moses with the life of Jesus provides a surprising number of similarities. Moses and Jesus were both born in dangerous times. Infants were being killed, but both of them were spared in unexpected ways. Neither of them seemed to have long-term relationships with their father. They were on Earth to bring freedom. Moses' freedom was political while Jesus' was spiritual. Both exhibited great love for the people but were rejected by many. Jesus and Moses spoke to very large groups (Matthew 5:1–2, Exodus 19:7). They also said some very important things to individuals. The most familiar verse in the Bible was said to a single individual (John 3:1–2, 16).

They both served a limited time but prepared others to minister after their deaths.

Jesus honored Moses and referred to him at least thirty-three times. Jesus clarified Moses' teaching at least six times. These were teachings that the religious leaders confused (Matthew 5:17, 27, 31, 33, 38, 43). The Gospel of John said the law was important, but grace fulfilled it.

> For the law was given through Moses; grace and truth came through Jesus Christ. (John 1:17)

> Therefore, holy brothers, who share in the heavenly calling, fix your thoughts on Jesus, the apostle and high priest whom we confess. He was faithful to the one who appointed him, just as Moses was faithful in all God's house. Jesus has been found worthy of greater honor than Moses. (Hebrews 3:1–3)

Chaplains can learn much from Moses. Chaplains can learn even more from Jesus. Jesus's actions speak loudly about his dealings with people. We can learn a great deal by studying the ways he related to others. Because he was a good listener, Jesus always seemed to know what other people were thinking. He also paid attention to the nonverbal signals. Chaplains cannot read people's minds, but they can listen carefully to those who share.

Jesus was patient as he taught those who genuinely sought to understand. Nicodemus and the Samaritan woman at the well are examples (John 3:1–15, 4:6).

Theological concepts are often hard to digest for inquirers and new Christians. Chaplains must allow time to patiently repeat explanations and perhaps provide appropriate reading material.

Jesus was compassionate with almost everyone, but he was harsh with religious leaders who thought they were better than other people. They were rebuked for their failure to properly apply the real meaning of the law. Some who tried to trap Jesus by his words were silenced by Jesus' rationale. Chaplains should carefully avoid anything that might give the impression that the chaplain thinks he or she is better or smarter than someone else.

Chaplains must strive to communicate caring concern. Rarely, it may be appropriate to confront someone who is hindering the ministry. During a worship service, a young couple was talking and giggling. I could hear it from the pulpit, and other worshipers were looking at them. After the benediction, while the congregation was filing out, I asked the couple to stay for a few minutes. After we had privacy, I expressed my concern with as much patience as I could muster. I told them that their behavior was inappropriate and distracting. I said they were welcome to attend worship anytime but only if they refrained from distracting others. After a few weeks absence, they returned and behaved appropriately.

Jesus was quick to forgive others and offer them a better life. The woman caught in adultery not only received forgiveness but also an opportunity for a better life. Jesus also used this encounter to strike out at hypocrisy (John 8:3–11).

Expressing judgment over someone's mistake will neutralize a chaplain's message. Expressing compassion will strengthen a chaplain's ministry as it builds relationships. Chaplains should offer reconciliation and hope.

Jesus allowed others to pursue their own spiritual pilgrimage even when it differed from his own. Pigs stampeding into the water and drowning made a powerful impression on those who saw it. Instead of recognizing the miraculous healing, they reacted with fear and asked Jesus to leave them. Though he might have criticized those people, he chose not to and simply went away (Matthew 8:28–34).

Most chaplains work in an interfaith environment. He or she cannot assume that there is common agreement in religious beliefs. The variety of religious practices can challenge even the most fair-minded chaplain. A balanced approach is needed but often hard to achieve. How can chaplains cooperate with other faiths without compromising their own beliefs. A few guidelines may help.

1. Do not criticize other people's beliefs or point out inconsistencies.
2. Do not push your own beliefs, but it is fair to answer questions if asked.
3. Remember, all faiths have some truth, none have all.
4. Distinguish between beliefs and practices when arranging events for other faith groups.
5. Be aware of the difference between direct pastoral services and coordinating other ministers' services.

A zealous hospice social worker wanted me to visit a patient who belonged to a group which strongly opposes my faith group. I told the social worker I would only visit if the patient invited me. After more urging from the social worker, the patient allowed me one visit but warned me in advance that she would correct my erroneous beliefs. Upon arrival, she launched into a twenty-minute recitation of why and how my faith was all wrong. Several times, she became loud and emotional. Some of her arguments were factually in error, but I decided it would be pointless to challenge her. Instead, when she stopped, I said, "Thank you for sharing. Now tell me about your family." She did and we became friends. She invited me to visit several more times.

CHAPTER 19

The Future of Chaplaincy

The conditions that required Moses' intervention in the ancient Israelite world are just as prevalent today. Cultural images are radically different, but basic human and spiritual needs remain the same. The needs are widespread and desperately needed. Today, people are enslaved by addictions of many kinds. Vast numbers of people are beaten down by poverty and discrimination imposed by society. Opportunities for advancement are denied to many because of race. Prisons are overcrowded. Medical care is less available and more expensive.

Chaplains cannot solve the problems of society. Jesus knew this when he said, "The poor you always have with you" (John 12:8). Ministry to individuals can ease some of this trauma. Chaplains are needed more than ever.

Some disturbing trends are evident. Some agencies are reducing the number of chaplains or eliminating them altogether. Some positions are being filled with untrained and unprepared persons. Volunteers who are untrained and unsupervised are being utilized more frequently. The important rigorous training needed for fully competent chaplains is being required less often. Chaplains are being employed who have not experienced CPE. Certification from professional organizations appears to be less important. Denominational endorsement is no longer required in some organizations.

I believe this is a serious matter. With each reduction of required credentials, chaplains lose opportunities for support, consultation, and networking. The effectiveness of the ministry is diminished.

We want our physicians to be board certified, our nurses to be licensed, our attorneys to be approved by the bar association, and our accountants to be certified. These crucial credentials are intended to ensure high standards of professionalism. Chaplain credentials are equally important and should be included in the qualifications for chaplains.

Chaplains should take advantage of occasions to emphasize the importance of chaplain ministry. Speaking to church groups, denominational agencies, and governmental agencies can be a good way to raise awareness of the importance of chaplain ministry and the importance of proper credentials.

CHAPTER 20

Some Personal Reflections

Throughout this book, you have seen that much of a chaplain's work has to do with problems. We minister to people in crisis. People are hurting physically and emotionally. People are fearful, often to the point of panic. People are confused and bewildered over questions that have no answers. Many questions are spiritual. People are lonely when families and friends withdraw because of their own discomfort.

Friends have sometimes felt sorry for me because of their perception that burdens shared are dragging me down. Sometimes, that happens, mostly not. The hospice example applies. I seldom feel depressed when observing people facing death. Instead, I am gratified when I see people face death with faith and comfort. A heartwarming experience emerges when families talk openly.

When I entered the hospital room of a terminally ill lady, she was crying. When asked, she said she was not upset over dying but because her family would not let her talk about it. "I only want to tell them it is okay." Being privileged to be included when people share their innermost thoughts can lead to fulfillment for a chaplain.

I offer a few suggestions of things that helped me to avoid being dragged down.

Remember,

> I am not responsible to fix everything.
> I do not need to have all the answers.
> I cannot heal broken relationships.
> I need not dwell on the negatives.

Instead,

> I must listen carefully and with care.
> I can recognize the ministry of presence. They will not remember what I said. They will remember that I was there.
> I should do my best with the time and resources I have and then leave it behind.

I feel a great deal of fulfillment from the ministry I have experienced. I am richly blessed. I thank God for the privilege of serving as a chaplain.

ENDNOTES

[1] Courtesy of Word Music, Nashville, TN, 1974,composed by Ken Medema

[2] Webster's Universal College Dictionary, 1997, Random House Inc., p 380

[3] The Qur'an Translation, translated by Abdullah Yusef Ali, Tahrike Tarsile Qu'ran Inc. New York, 2011, p. 520

[4] Life Magazine, Time Inc. New York, Vol. 18, No.5, March 2018, p. 4

[5] Personal notes taken from a conference for military psychiatrists and chaplains, The Menninger Clinic, Topeka, KS, approximately 1985

[6] Josephus, Antiquities, translated by William Whiston A.M. Hendrickson Publishers, Peabody, Massachusetts, 1987 & 2004, p. 68

[7] Phillip Swanson, Biblical Illustrator, Sunday School Board of the Southern Baptist Convention, spring 1994, p. 3 & 7

[8] William Lasor, Great Personalities of the Old Testament, Fleming Revell Co. 1959, p. 56–57

[9] Army Chaplain Corps Activities—AR 165-1, United States Government, 2005, p. 1

[10] Ibid, p. 45

[11] Ibid, p. 7

[12] Swindoll, Charles R., Moses: God's Man for a Crisis, Insight for Living Publishing, 1985, p. 19

[13] The Association for Clinical Pastoral Education, 55 Ivan Allen Jr. Blvd. Suite 835, Atlanta, GA 30308, 404-320-1472, acpe@acpe.edu.

[14] Chaplain Carl Hart, quoted in Home Missions Magazine, published by The Home Mission Board of the Southern Baptist Convention, vol. XLIII, Atlanta, GA, Nov. 1972, p. 19

[15] Rick Davies, Biblical Illustrator, Sunday School Board of the Southern Baptist Convention, Nashville, TN, 1962, p. 72

[16] J. Pederson, quoted in G. Henton Davies, The Interpreter's Dictionary of the Bible, Vol. 2, Abingdon Press, p. 72

[17] Raymond Abba, The Interpreter's Dictionary of the Bible, Vol. 3, Abington Press, Nashville, TN, p. 877–881

[18] Army Chaplain Corps Activities—AR165-1, United States Government, 2015, section 16-2, p. 45

ABOUT THE AUTHOR

Kenneth W. Cook is a retired chaplain having served in ministry for over fifty years. He served in nine different settings in four states. He earned a BA from Mercer University, an MDiv from Midwestern Baptist Seminary, and a DMin from Southern Baptist Seminary. He advanced to the rank of colonel in the US Army Reserve. Ken and Martha (Thrasher) have been married for over sixty-four years and enjoy their children, grandchildren, and great-grandchildren. They live in a retirement community near Birmingham, Alabama. Ken enjoys making Christmas tree ornaments and crosses to give away.